Enter into among between your toes as you make your way to the cool water of the fishin' hole. Catch the scent of sweet magnolias as the lazy afternoon breeze wafts through the trees. Come along with Jim Rogers as he relives his childhood days:

...a big sow came oink-oink-oinking toward the hole in the fence. I dropped an ear to the ground. When the sow squeezed under the fence to get the corn, I dropped on her back. She tore out bucking and squealing across the pasture with me riding backward and cranking her tail.

A shock like a bolt of electricity raced through my body so powerfully it caused my fingers and toes to tingle. I felt a jolt and then a stabbing pain in my chest. Black Breed and I stared at each other, he surprised and I frozen in fear.

Goober turned to me with a desperate look in his eyes but no sniveling appeal could compensate for my shattered dreams. I wasn't going to be interviewed by all those reporters, after all. No gold coins were going to trickle through my fingers. I'd have to work hard for every Orange Crush I'd ever drink.

In Care of the Conductor

To Dr. B. White

with

Best Regards

Jim Rogue

Copyright Jim Rogers
First Printing June 1994
ISBN 0-929292-76-6
Library of Congress 94-076803

All Rights Reserved
Printed in the United States of America
by Lithocolor Press, Inc.
Cover Design by Cyndi Allison
(Use coupon in back of book to order extra copies of this and other books
from Hannibal Books.)

Dedicated to my dear wife, Laura.

Foreword

by James C. Hefley

Author of *Way Back in the Hills*.

When I first met genial Jim Rogers, I knew we had much in common. "Ah'm from Newton County," he grinned, "where we said 'foah' and 'yoah.' In east central Mississippi, between Jackson and Meridian, where the sweet magnolia blooms."

"And I'm from Newton County, Arkansas," I countered, "where we said 'fer' and 'yer.' Our cornfield leaned so steep that Daddy had to prop up the plowhorse to keep him from rolling off the mountain."

More talk revealed that our growing-up years were both alike and different.

We both loved to fish. Jim snagged more catfish. I hooked more bass.

We both grew up on farms during the same Great Depression, although neither of us saw the times as hard. That, we agreed, was because we had caring loved ones who looked after us and always saw that we had something to eat, even if it was just cornbread and milk.

I was blessed with two loving parents and a host of relatives who lived in the same mountain valley. My daddy was always there to take me coon hunting and fishing.

Jim never saw his father when he was growing up. "I found out years later," Jim told me, "that he lay in the arms of another woman, on the night my mother gave birth to me."

I am the oldest of eight. My Newton County was the only county in Arkansas not to ever have a foot of railroad track.

Jim is an only child who spent most of his boyhood with his grandparents and uncles and aunts. To visit his waitress mother in St. Louis, Jim rode the Mobile & Ohio train, with the protective tag, "IN CARE OF THE CONDUCTOR," looped around his neck.

So comes the title of Jim's true story, for the railroad officer was only one of many "conductors" who guided Jim along the railway of life.

This book, which I encouraged him to write, is Jim's "legacy" to his grandchildren, as my book is to mine.

I'm proud to be his publisher. I love his story. If you liked my book *Way Back in the Hills* you'll love *In Care of the Conductor*.

Table of Contents

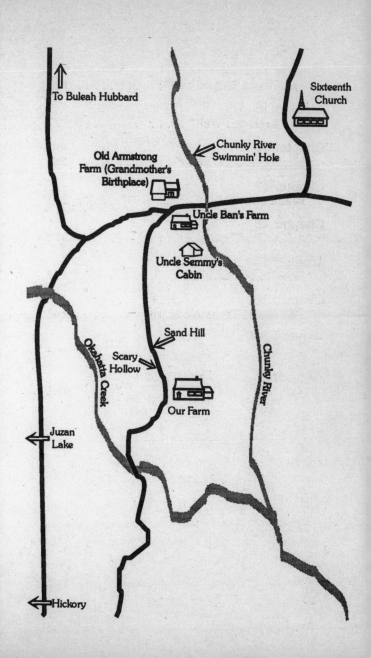

Chapter 1

"Red-Headed Chicken Squeezer"

On the hot and sticky night of July 31, 1924, a thin, young blonde woman moaned on a sweat-soaked bed in a French style farm house, three miles out from the town of Hickory, in Newton County, Mississippi. Barely twenty and only five feet tall, she rolled her head from side to side, biting her lips at the pain that racked her body, as her mother and the physician hovered over her under the light of a kerosene lamp.

Dr. Clarence Vernon Gilmore, in a rumpled seersucker suit and black string tie, pursed his lips under his tobacco-streaked moustache. He glanced across the bed to the older woman who kept wiping the sweat from her daughter Ruth's face. "Cain't be too much longah now, Miz Jennie," the doctor assured.

Grandmother tried to encourage her oldest daughter. "Honey, you've gotta keep on strainin' an' pushin'. C'mon, yuh can do it!"

A deep groan, a scream, and I slipped into Dr. Gilmore's sensitive hands. A quick tie, a snip, and a soft pat on my bottom, and he gently placed me in the waiting blanket held up by Grandmother. "Heah, Miz Jennie," the doctor instructed, "clean this chile up while Ah take care uv Mama Ruth."

My grandfather — the man I would call "Daddy Floyd," my two teenage uncles, and my two young aunts slept through it all. Grandmother tenderly folded the blanket about her first grandchild and carried me to the black woman waiting in the kitchen. "Lizzie, jus' take a look at what Ruth gave us."

"Aunt Lizzie" craned her neck to see the new arrival. A slow smile enveloped her sharply chiseled dark face. "Lawsey me, Miz Jennie, he sho am white — an' pink too. An' lookit that red haah. He cudden be no purtiah lessen he be black. My, my, my. Miz Ruth sho mus' be proud uv 'im."

Grandmother grinned at her black maid. "Lizzie, Ah don't think Ruth even knows he's heah yet. Doctor Gilmore is tendin' her now."

Aunt Lizzie reached for the blanket. "Gimme the young'un, Miz Jennie an' Ah'll wash 'im off. You go on back an' hep the doctah."

Grandmother smiled in gratitude and passed me over. "Thank yuh, Lizzie. Poor Ruth is gonna need all the care she can get."

Dr. Gilmore later warned Mother, "Ruth, you'ah plain too liddle to be havin' babies. The nex'un might kill yuh."

I would be her only child.

Mother scribbled James Charles Rogers on my birth certificate. Born the same day as a future president, I would be called Jimmie, requiring me to explain time and again, "No, Ah'm not related to that yodeler from Meridian, Mississippi. He's Jimmie Ro-D-gers. Ah'm Rogers without the D."

Mother had been working as a waitress and living with my father in St. Louis. Her decision to come back to Mississippi and give birth at home had been triggered by reading a story in **The St. Louis Star-Times** about the switching of babies in a hospital. She was even more afraid that she might be given a redhead like her father-in-law whom she detested. So she caught the Mobile & Ohio express south to Meridian where her father picked her up at the depot and brought her to the farm where she'd been raised as a child.

Naturally I turned out to be a redhead.

My father didn't visit, write, send a small present, or ever provide any child support. He did nothing to acknowledge my birth and express pride in his offspring. Indeed, he was in bed with one of Mother's girl friends on the night I was born.

After twelve long weeks of rest, Mother asked her parents to take her back to Meridian, where she and I would catch the Mobile & Ohio north back to St. Louis. "Ah'm gonna try to get my waitress job back an' hold mah marriage together," she said.

Her hopes were dashed. A year later my father skipped town in the dead of night with Mother's old girl friend. I wouldn't see him again until I was almost 30 years old.

Mother packed her few belongings and carried me back on the train. Daddy Floyd and Grandmother met us at the station in Meridian and took us home with them. "Everything's goin' to be awl right, Ruth," Grandmother kept assuring Mother. "You can jus' rest a little more with us while you'ah decidin' what to do next."

Mother wanted to pay for her keep. She tried substitute teaching in the Hickory School, about three miles from the farm, hoping to step into a permanent position. When it became obvious that this might be years, she took her meager savings and opened a small restaurant in town.

Hickory was then a thriving farm community of around 700 with three cotton gins, a grist mill and a huge sawmill. Mother was sure she could make it in business. As for Daddy Floyd and Grandmother, they couldn't be happier to have Mother and their first grandson at home.

We settled into farm life and the family circle. Daddy Floyd and Grandmother's big white house, built New Orleans style, had only three bedrooms, but they were each more than 20 feet square, with a fireplace in each room. My two teenage uncles, Cecil and Vernell, slept in the boys' room across the wide hall. Mother and my Aunt Helen Maude — only six years old — occupied the double bed in the girls' room where I was born. I was tucked away in a crib on Mother's side of the bed. Two-year-old Aunt Doris, Mother's youngest sibling, slept in a crib at the foot of Daddy Floyd and Grandmother's bed.

As soon as I got old enough to walk, they let me play in the back yard with the chickens. Round and round I chased the clucking hens and stately red roosters. Pant, pant. Cluck, cluck. Pant, pant. Cluck,

cluck. I couldn't catch a hen or rooster, but the chicks were a different story. I grabbed one and held it close, so close that I squeezed the life out of it. That was only the first one.

Grandmother couldn't figure out what or who was killing her chicks. One afternoon she caught me red-handed. "Jimmie, put down that baby chick!" Aunt Lizzie came running into the backyard. "Lawsy me, that chile's the varmint that's been killin' the babies."

Mother was working eighteen hour days, trying to keep her restaurant going. She heard about my acts the next morning. "Jimmie, did yuh kill yoah grandmothah's chickens?"

I twisted and squirmed and finally nodded my head.

Mother looked sadly at me. "You'ah not to squeeze the poah little chickens again yuh heah?"

"Uh, huh. Won't squeeze any moah chickies."

Mother couldn't bring herself to spank me. But when I killed another one, she tried a more drastic tactic.

I was in the yard chasing chicks, when I heard a "woo-woo-woo" coming down the road. I looked and saw a white-sheeted apparition, flapping its arms like a monstrous fowl, coming straight at me.

"Woo-woo-woo! Woo-woo-woo! Chicken Man's gonna get yuh."

I stopped dead in my tracks. My muscles froze and I fell face down in the dirt, too breathless to scream.

Still wearing the white sheet, Mother rushed to my aid. Grandmother and Aunt Lizzie came charging out of the house. They had to turn me on my back and apply artificial respiration to get me breathing again.

Mother learned a lesson and so did I. I never squeezed another chicken, and she never tried to scare me again.

By this time I was aware that the man I called Daddy Floyd was not my father. Although Mother didn't talk about him, I knew he was living somewhere. As I played back and forth around the farm, I frequently glanced across the fields to where the road came up from the swamp and passed by the piney woods on its way up the piney slope to where it ran by our house. This was the direction from which my dad would come. I fantasized seeing his car rising from the swampy lowland, followed by a cloud of dust, on his way to see me. But he never came.

Dear Mother. She put heart and soul into her restaurant business. She always had a ready smile and was fast and efficient at everything she did. But in the late 1920's when farm product prices were dropping, few people could afford to eat out.

She and my grandparents kept hoping the economy would pick up. Instead, things got worse. The year I was four over 500 banks failed in the United States. The next year, 1929, the bottom fell out of the stock market. Millions lost their jobs, savings and homes. We heard of people jumping out of office windows and committing suicide. Daddy

Floyd and Grandmother sat staring at the front page of the **Meridian Star**, shaking their heads at news of more business failures and suicides. "Thank God, we'ah not in debt," Daddy Floyd said, "or we'd prob'ly lose ouah farm, too."

Mother was working from sunup to midnight, still trying to scratch out a living for herself and her son. Daddy Floyd took her to work before I woke up. When her brother, Cecil wasn't available, my grandfather went back after her at night.

One evening, after falling asleep beside my Uncle Vernell, I awoke to hear Mother, Daddy Floyd and Grandmother talking. Mother was crying. "Mothah, Daddy," I heard her moan, "Ah'm, jus' at mah wit's end. Ah can buy food dirt cheap from farmers, but nobody can afford mah cookin'. Ah've tried, Lord knows Ah've tried. Ah'm so tired at night, Ah jus' fall in bed. An' Ah hardly evah see mah little Jimmie." Her voice trailed off in sobs.

"Theah, theah, darlin'," Daddy Floyd assured. "It's gonna be all right. You've got a home with us as long as yuh want to stay."

"Ah know that, Daddy. But Ah've got a foah-yeah-old son to bring up. It's not fair for yuh and Mama to have all that responsibility."

Grandmother's tearful voice broke in. "Honey, youah little boy isn't any trouble. We love him like he's ouah own son."

There came a long pause, then I heard Mother again. "Ah don't want yuh awl to think Ah'm a quittah, but Ah jus' cain't keep mah liddle restaurant open much longah."

I pictured Grandmother folding Mother in her arms, as she said, "Now lissen to me, Ruth, you'ah a grown woman. The Lord's goin' to provide for you and Jimmie. If not through us, then theah'll be anothah way."

Not long after that a friend wrote Mother about a waitress job in Memphis, Mother said she'd take it. She sold her fixtures and equipment for the price of a train ticket and little more. "Jimmie," she whispered, pressing me tight and ruffling my red hair, "Ah'm goin' ta leave yuh with youah Daddy Floyd an' Grandmothah foah a little while. They'll take good care of yuh. Yuh be a good boy, an' Ah'll be back foah yuh 'fo you know it."

Daddy Floyd backed his '27 Ford open touring sedan out of the garage. "Take a picture uv me an' Jimmie 'fo Ah leave," Mother implored Grandmother. Mother seated herself on the brick pillar beside the front porch steps. I stood behind her in short pants and Grandmother took her old box camera and snapped the photo.

"Time to go, evahbody," Daddy Floyd reminded. Grandmother and Mother climbed in the front. Helen Maude, Doris and I hopped in the back. My uncles, Cecil and Vernell, had jobs.

In 1929 Highway 80 hadn't yet been built. Daddy Floyd had to drive the twenty-five miles east to Meridian through the Chunky River swamp. The dirt road ran between water-filled ditches. It wasn't muddy, but still moist and slippery and he kept wrestling the steering wheel to keep out of the deep ruts left by vehicles during and after the last heavy rain.

Thunk! The front wheels dropped to the bottom of a rut with a bone jarring crunch. Daddy Floyd geared down and gunned the engine. The car bounced out. Hanging on to the wheel, my grandfather kept twisting and shifting until he got on level ground. Finally we pulled out of the swamp and put-putted into the low range of hills approaching Meridian.

I was nearing my fifth birthday. Aunt Doris, almost six, tried to act as a grown-up tour guide. "Jimmie! Jimmie! Look, theah's Burrell Springs."

I wiggled off Mother's lap and raked Helen Maude's legs getting to the other side of the car. "Wheah's a girl spring, Doris?" I squealed.

Doris laughed. "No, silly. Not a girl spring. Burrell Springs."

Then, over to the left, I saw a figure come flashing down the steep hillside riding a wooden sled. The sled hit the end of the slide and soared 30 feet over the water, then skipped repeatedly another 40 feet before settling in the water. "Whoooie!" the sled rider hollered, splashing with his arms. A thousand questions tumbled from my lips as Daddy Floyd sped on towards Meridian.

A little ways on we stopped at a hamburger stand, owned by Uncle Ban Allen's brother. Uncle Ban was married to Grandmother's sister, Aunt Maggie. They lived about a mile from Daddy Floyd's farm.

Daddy Floyd bought a sackful and handed the burgers to Mother. "Take these san'wiches, Honey, an' heah's a dollah 'fo some pop on the way."

"But Daddy," she protested. "That's a lot uv money. Ah can drink watah."

Daddy Floyd made her keep the dollar bill anyway.

Mother was now crying with me reaching to wipe the tears from her eyes. She kept saying, "I'll send foah yuh, Jimmie. I'll send foah yuh, little dahlin'." I last saw her peering at us through the train window, clutching her handkerchief tightly over her mouth and waving slowly as the locomotive huffed away from the station.

I wailed loud and long, "Mothah! Mothah! Ah wants mah mothah!"

"Let's go," Daddy Floyd summoned.

Leading me by the hand, Grandmother followed Daddy Floyd to the car. Doris skipped along beside us and Helen Maude brought up the rear.

I kept sobbing for my mother.

Chapter 2

"School Daze"

Mother was as good as her word. A couple of months later, in late August, 1929, Daddy Floyd and Grandmother put me on the Mobile & Ohio train with a tag tied to my collar button inscribed "IN CARE OF THE CONDUCTOR."

In those days travelling alone was considered safe for children. "You'll be fine, Jimmie," Daddy Floyd assured. "The conductor will watch over yuh an' youah mothah will meet yuh in Memphis."

I didn't feel afraid at all. The passengers made a fuss over me and stuffed me with cookies and candy to the brink of nausea. It didn't seem long until the train pulled into the barn-like Memphis station. I spotted a slim, blonde lady on the platform and bounced on my seat. "Mothah! Mothah! It's me!" I shouted, even though she couldn't hear. "It's Jimmie!"

Mother saw me and began jumping up and down. The passengers smiled and laughed. "Let the little boy off first," they told the conductor.

The conductor raised the trap door that covered the steps. I pushed past him and dived into Mother's arms. There in the smoke and falling cinders, completely oblivious to the crowd around us, Mother cascaded tears and kisses over my head and cheeks.

"Oh, Mothah, Ah mis't yuh so much," I sobbed.

"Ah know, baby, Ah know, an' Ah mis't yuh so bad Ah thought Ah'd jus' die. But you ah with me now an' foahevah."

I attended kindergarten in Memphis. Today my only Memphis memories are of the teacher who sat me on her lap on a trip one night to see the brightly-lighted stern-wheelers and side-wheelers pass in parade on the Mississippi. At the end of the school year, Mother packed a bag of sandwiches and took me to the train where they tied on my tag, "IN CARE OF THE CONDUCTOR." Daddy Floyd, Grandmother, Helen Maude and Doris met me at the Meridian station.

During that summer, while I was on the farm, Mother moved back north to St. Louis where she found another waitress job. "Ship Jimmie up here for the school year," she wrote Daddy Floyd and Grandmother. "I'll be responsible for him."

In late August of my seventh year, when the Meridian blues singer Jimmie Rodgers was making more money than President Hoover, Daddy Floyd cranked up the old Ford and we were off to Meridian again. He stopped and bought me a bag of hamburgers from Uncle Ban's brother, then drove on to the depot.

Grandmother could bend her emotions to her will, and Doris was very much like her. Daddy Floyd cried openly and unashamedly. "Jimmie, boy," he sobbed, "the Lawd knows we'ah gonna miss yuh." Helen Maude clung to Daddy Floyd and matched him sob for sob. I kissed them all over and over and then ran up the steps to the passenger car. At the top I turned to wave and emotion suddenly constricted my chest. Dashing back down, I hugged them all again.

"Come back to us, yuh heah, boy? Come back real soon," cried Daddy Floyd as he wiped away a flood of tears.

The lonesome whistle blew. "Bo'ahd. All abo'ahd!" a voice called. The uniformed man reached for my hand and led me inside the car where he attached the tag, "IN CARE OF THE CONDUCTOR." As the train chugged out of the station, I waved to Daddy Floyd, Grandmother, Doris and Helen Maude until they were out of sight.

Mother met me at the big Union Station in St. Louis. We got on a bus with my bags and rode to a stop near her boarding house. I bounded up the stairs behind her to her third floor, single room, which with kitchen privileges was all she could afford. After she unpacked my things we had a soup supper, then she gently tucked me in bed and climbed in beside me. I fell asleep in her arms.

The next day was Sunday and Mother took me to the St. Louis Zoo. I clapped and danced at seeing my first elephant. I growled at the tigers and turned handsprings before the monkey cage. We enjoyed a good lunch and then got back on the transit bus.

I assumed that I would be spending the night again with Mother. Instead, she began stuffing clothes back into my bag.

"Ah'm goin' back to the fahm?"

"Not today, Jimmie," she said. "When I get some more time off, we'll go visit Daddy Floyd and your grandmothah. This evenin' we'ah goin' to meet the lady who you'll be boardin' with while yuh go to school.

My eyes welled up with tears. "Ah'm not goin' ta be livin' with yuh?"

She held a brave face. "I live too fah from your school. You'll be stayin' with a real nice lady. Ah'll come and get yuh on Saturday an' we'll go places together."

Carrying my bag in one hand, she led me back to the bus stop. I sobbed all the way. "Mothah, Ah wanna stay with yuh. Mothah, can't yuh keep me. Ah'll be good. Ah won't cause yuh no trouble."

The bus pulled up. Mother gently pushed me ahead of her, as she followed, carrying my bag. Finally, after an interminably long ride, she said, "This is wheah we get off." She took me by the hand and led me down the steps of the bus. I started crying again. "Ah wanna go back to youah house. Take me back. Ah don't wanna be left with a strangah."

Mother dragged me down the long block and turned up a walkway to a white frame bungalow. Further down the street, I saw a red-brick building.

"This is wheah you'll be stayin'. You'll be real close to youah school. It's right down theah," she pointed.

I pulled on her hand. "Mothah, take me back home with yuh. I don't wanna leave yuh. Please, Mothah. Please." I began wailing.

Mother knelt down and looked directly into my eyes. "Jimmie, you'ah a big boy now. Remember, Ah'll be back Saturday. Ah promise."

I swallowed hard. She dabbed at my eyes with her handkerchief. I saw the door open. A buxom white lady with long brown hair emerged from the house. "Come on in," she gushed in a crisp northern accent. "I'm Mrs. Kaiser and you must be Jimmie. Your mama has told me lots of good things about you."

After more talk, she directed us to my room where Mother put my clothes into two dresser drawers. "Now let's go have a look at your school," Mother said.

We walked all around the red brick building. Mother took me over to a window and pointed inside. "This is your classroom. Your teacher is Miss Burt. She's a real nice lady. She knows you'll be coming tomorrow.

I kept my composure until we got back to Mrs. Kaiser's house. There I started wailing again. Mother bent down and gave me another talking and wiped away the tears. Then she took me up to my room.

"Mind Miz Kaiser, jus' like yuh would me," Mother ordered gently. "Ah'll see yuh next Saturday. That's mah day off."

Mother walked over to Mrs. Kaiser. "Heah's the phone number wheah I work, in case of an emergency."

She turned and took me in her arms. I leaned my head against her shoulder and sobbed. She pulled my hands away and gently set me down. Then she turned and walked through the door. I ran after her, shrieking, "Mothah, take me with yuh. Mothah, please take me."

Mrs. Kaiser grasped me firmly by the arm. "She'll be back, Jimmie. She'll be back."

I cried myself to sleep that first night. Later I learned, that to help pay for my room and board, Mother walked to and from her waitress job each day, a distance of over a mile each way. A ride on the city bus cost only a nickel in 1931, but a savings of a dime a day was worth walking two miles to her. Her weekly pay, including tips, was no more than seven or eight dollars a week. With no hope of my father coming back, she had filed for divorce.

I survived the week. I cried the first day of school until Miss Burt, the pretty, blonde first grade teacher, took me on her lap. "Teacher's pet," a girl chirped, and I jumped down and ran to my seat. The second day wasn't so bad and by Friday I'd even made a couple of friends.

Saturday morning, as soon as I could escape from Mrs. Kaiser's breakfast table, I hurried to the porch to watch for mother. When I saw her coming, I ran to meet her, arms outstretched for her loving embrace.

She hugged me tight, sat me down, and asked about school. Then she said, "We're gonna have fun today, Jimmie. My customers gave me good tips this week, so we can go to the Highlands Amusement Park an' ride the rollah coastah." As she rattled off all she'd planned for us to do, I clapped my hands in glee.

The best part of the day was going home with Mother. The sad part came the next morning when she took me back to Mrs. Kaiser's. "Ah have to be at work by noon," she explained. "You can walk me to the bus stop and wait with me for the bus."

The bus pulled up in about ten minutes. I started to cry again. Mother hugged me tight and forced a smile. "Be a big boy for your mothah," she said. "Remember, I'll be back, Saturday."

"Yuh won't forget me?"

"No, I won't foahget you, darlin'."

She stepped into the bus, turned and blew me a kiss. I ran after her until the bus turned the corner at the end of the street and disappeared. Then I shuffled back to my lodgings.

The schedule became for me a routine. Saturdays, I sat on the porch, watching for Mother. When she came in sight, I ran to meet her with open arms. She asked about school, then let me display my learning. "Oh, Ah'm so proud of you, Jimmie," she said. "Yuh brighten up mah whole week."

Our parting on Sunday always came hard. I cried bitter tears at the bus stop and hung on to her neck until she had to twist my arms away. "Ah'll be back, next Saturday," she assured. "You be a good boy and do yoah lessons." Then the bus pulled up and she was gone.

About six weeks into the school term, Mrs. Kaiser began fussing at me. "Jimmie, can't you ever get downstairs to breakfast on time?"

"Ah'm sorry, Miz Kaiser. Ah won't be late again."

The next time I was late she screamed, "If you're not down here in five minutes, young man, you'll go to school without anything to eat!"

Shirt tail flapping, I raced into the dining room.

"Get to the table!" she yelled.

When I hesitated, she grabbed me around the waist, lifted me bodily, and slammed me down on the chair. I burst into tears.

She yelled louder. "Shut up, or you'll really get it!"

Fortunately, the next day was Saturday. When Mother arrived for her visit, my bottom was still sore. She saw me walking stiffly and asked, "What's the mattuh?"

"Miz Kaiser pushed me down on the chair in the dining room. It hurt!" I began crying again.

Mother had words with Mrs. Kaiser. When things didn't get better, Mother moved me to a another boarding house a couple of blocks away. Mrs. Bogan, a smiling, gray-haired grandmother, cared for me like I was one of her own. I settled back into the normal routine of counting the days until Saturday.

Finally, Mother realized that I needed a more stable life. When she came to get me at the end of my first school year, she asked, "How would you like to stay with Daddy Floyd and Grandmothah and go to school in Hickory all year long?"

I had been looking forward to spending the summer at the farm. I couldn't think of anything better than staying on. Then a tear trickled down my face. "But when will Ah see you?"

"Oh, Ah'll come down and visit when the boss gives me some time off, and you can come on the train to see me. We won't forget each othah, will we?"

I shook my red head, fighting back more tears.

Mother saw me on the south bound Mobile & Ohio. The conductor greeted me warmly and affixed the identification to my collar button. The whistle blew and the train began pulling away....Chug — — —chug — — -chug — — chug — chug-chu g-chug... I settled back in my seat for the trip south. While I felt sad at leaving Mother, I could hardly wait to see Daddy Floyd, Grandmother, my aunts and uncles and all the animals at the farm again.

Fourteen hours later the train rolled into the Meridian station. I was already down the aisle when the conductor came to open the door. I ripped the tag from my shirt and threw it on the floor. My heart pounded as I waited impatiently in the aisle.

"Watch your feet, son," the conductor cautioned when he opened the door.

Daddy Floyd was waiting at the foot of the steps. I leaped into his arms and hugged him, then reached for Grandmother. Helen Maude gave me a smack, but Doris who was now nine, merely tossed her straight blonde hair and chirped, "Hey, Jimmie. Have yuh killed any moah chickens?"

I took a comforting deep breath. I had missed her too.

Daddy Floyd got my bags and cranked the Ford. Grandmother put me in front with her and Daddy Floyd and the girls climbed in back.

I asked about my uncles, Vernell and Cecil. "They'ah away workin'," Grandmother said. "They'll be home foah a visit nex' weekend."

We headed back to the farmhouse where I was born.

Chapter 3

"Snake in the Corn Crib"

All that summer Mother wrote almost every week. I often sat on the porch listening for the put-put of the mailman's Model T. Grandmother — when she wasn't workin' in the field — would come trooping out for the mail while I danced along beside her expectantly.

She'd thumb through envelopes and say, "No, Jimmie, we didn't get a letter from youah Mama, today. Prob'ly we will tomorrow. You'll jus' have to be patient."

Or, "Well, look uh heah, boy, Mistuh Hambrick brought us a lettah from youah mothah." Then I'd jump and squeal. "Let me hold it, Grandmothah."

Grandmother would let me feel it, then she'd read parts of Mother's letter aloud, skipping over things which she thought might be worrisome to me or Doris who hung nearby listening. Grandmother always made sure I heard Mother's reminder: "Mind Daddy Floyd and Grandmother and help with the chores. And don't get into any fusses with Doris."

By and by, as the summer wore on, I became less anxious about Mother. Some days I actually forgot to ask if a letter had come from her. As for my father, I still held out hope that someday he would come zooming up the clay hill in a dazzling roadster and sweep me up into his arms. But as time slipped by I thought of him less and less.

The boarding house in St. Louis was a distant memory. My grandparents' farm was now my home, the surrounding pastures, swamps and creeks my playground. We all had chores, but there were always interesting things to do and challenges to meet.

Take the time when I was in the hallway of our house and heard Daddy Floyd talking to Grandmother in the kitchen. I edged up close to grab every word.

"Jennie, yuh better tell Jimmie to stay away from the corn crib," Daddy Floyd was saying. "Ah put a big ole king snake in theah to catch the rats."

Grandmother quickly answered, "Ah'll tell him an' yuh can jus' count on bringin' out the corn foah the chickens youahself."

Peeping through a crack in the door, I saw Daddy Floyd 's mouth spread in a big smile as He grabbed Grandmother in a playful embrace. "Come out to the corn crib with me, Jennie. Ah'll show yuh that ole friendly king snake.

"No thank yuh," Grandmother declared.

Daddy Floyd flopped his big hat on his head and laughed. "Ah'll be in mah shop, if yuh decide to change youah mind."

I slipped quietly down the hall and out the front screen door, taking care not to let it slam. I skittered over to the barn. I knew I had to hurry before I was seen and told not to go there.

I stepped into the passageway that separated the crib from the stables, carefully avoiding fresh piles of manure left by cows taking shelter from a recent rainstorm. The doorway to the crib was boarded up almost to the top. Daddy Floyd had added boards as the crib was filled during the harvest, then cut toehold steps so he could climb to the top and pull out corn ears.

I didn't care for snakes at all, but I was irresistibly drawn to Daddy Floyd's corn crib like a moth to a flame. Cautiously, I edged up the steps to where I could peer over the top board.

The sun filtered through ventilating slats in the side of the crib. Sloooowly and caaarefully, I swung my head around and saw only yellow corn piled in all directions. Disappointed and yet relieved, I took a long, deep breath and let it out. Somehow I felt I had passed some sort of test for bravery.

Then I stuck my head further into the opening to check the left side of the doorway. There, not six inches in front of my nose was the biggest snake I'd ever seen! The huge reptile flicked out its tongue, almost under my nose. My eyelids popped so wide they hurt. I tried to scream and couldn't. My throat froze tight. I sought to straighten out my fingertips that clutched the top board and fell backwards to the barn floor with a bone jarring, squishy thump.

Without waiting to see if my back was broken, I jumped up and raced out of the barn. The ten-foot board fence around the barn didn't slow me down a bit. I must have sailed over that fence as I ran shrieking toward Daddy Floyd's shop, located across the road from the front of the house.

Daddy Floyd came running out and grabbed me with hands still warm from working at his forge. "Yech! Thunderation!" He dropped me in a limp heap on the ground and yelled for Grandmother. "Jennie, oh, Jennie. Come an' clean the stinkin' manure off this boy."

My grandfather strode toward the wash stand on the back porch, stripping off his shirt as he walked, leaving me lying in the middle of the road feeling deserted. Daddy Floyd would have defended me to his death, but not if I was covered with fresh cow manure.

Grandmother came tearing out of the house, with Aunt Lizzie sprinting behind her. "Good heavens, Jimmie, how'd yuh get into that — "?

Grandmother quickly took charge of the messy situation. "Floyd, get me a tub of water. Lizzie, oh, Lizzie bring me some big wash cloths. Jimmie, yuh stay right where yuh are, boy."

Doris had been playing paper dolls in the backyard. Helen Maude had fallen asleep reading a book. Both came running to see what all the commotion was about.

Doris took one look and grabbed her nose. "Jimmie fell in cow plop."

Grandmother directed Doris and Helen Maude back into the house, "and don't peep," she added, "till we get some clean clothes on Jimmie."

Daddy Floyd lugged the wash tub over to where I was lying in the road. Grandmother and Aunt Lizzie stripped off my clothes, washed away the manure and checked to see if I had any bruises. "Looks like the manure cushioned his fall. Lizzie, get him some clean clothes," Grandmother ordered.

"Boy, how did yuh get in such a stink?" Daddy Floyd asked, covering a snicker with the back of his hand.

"Ah, uh, Ah was playin' in the barn an' fell from the corn crib."

Grandmother, who didn't get mad very often, turned on Daddy Floyd. "Floyd, that snake yuh put in the crib could uv bit Jimmie. Didn't yuh tell him about it?"

Daddy Floyd's chuckle died in his mouth. "No, but — "

"He could have gotten poisoned."

"Jennie, a king snake isn't poisonous."

"No mattah. It could give the boy nightmares foah a year. Nex' time, yuh tell 'im, Floyd."

All Daddy Floyd said was, "Boy, come with me to the shop. Ah'll find somethin' for yuh to do that'll keep you out of trouble."

I never did tell that I had heard them talking about the snake before going to the barn.

And Doris never got tired of holding her nose when she saw me coming out of the barn.

Chapter 4

"Ride 'em Hog-boy!"

One sunny afternoon Daddy Floyd and I drove into Hickory. The whole town seemed subdued. "Who died?" Daddy Floyd asked.

"Didn't you hear the news over the radio?" the hardware store man asked.

"We don't have a radio."

"Well, Jimmie Rodgers died in New York City. Hemorrhaged to death. Drowned in his own blood, the radio fellah reported. Theah' bringing him back to Meridian in a special railroad car. Theah' 'spectin' a big crowd to be at the station when the train rolls in this evenin'."

Nobody from our family went, but we heard later that hundreds came to welcome the alcoholic blues singer home.

Mother came to see us for Thanksgiving, saying she could only stay two days. "That's all the time my boss will let me have off," she explained. "These are hard times. With so many people out of work, Ah'm just thankful to have a waitress job."

I heard them talking about more bank closings and a new government program called The New Deal. "Times ah' bad, real bad," Daddy Floyd said. "Ah've never seen so many people down and out."

Daddy Floyd cranked up his '27 Ford to take Mother to the Meridian station. Mother told us all goodbye, then bent down and hugged me tight. Our tears blended as she sobbed, "Oh, Jimmie, my dahlin' boy. Ah already miss you so much Ah can hahdly stand it. One day, one day, Ah'm gonna marry the man of mah dreams. We'll have a fine house and you'll come and live with me where you belong."

"When, Mothah? When?"

"One day," she promised. "Till then, yuh be a good boy for Daddy Floyd and Grandmother. Ah'll be back to see yuh, real soon."

After Mother left I began thinking about Christmas. Daddy Floyd and Grandmother couldn't afford store-bought decorations for the tree my uncles dragged in from the piney woods. We dipped popcorn in molasses and strung it around the tree on sewing thread alongside paper chains and home-made ornaments.

We kept hoping Mother would be able to come for Christmas until a package containing a letter and a little twenty-five cent harmonica for me arrived two days before the holiday. "I'd give anything to be with you, Jimmie, and the rest of the family," she wrote, "but my boss can't spare me the time off. I hope to get down for Easter. We'll see."

When she was unable to come for Easter, plans were made for me to visit her for a few days when school was out. On the Tuesday following, Daddy Floyd and the family took me to Meridian where I boarded the familiar north-bound Mobile & Ohio. The conductor came to string his "IN CARE OF..." sign on my collar button. "Ah'm eight years old, an Ah don't need that," I protested. He shook his head. "Yuh gotta have it, son. It's the rule."

Mother met me with hugs and kisses at the St. Louis station. "Mothah," I said, "after we talked a bit, you talk funny. You say 'I' instead of 'Ah'."

She smiled. "Do I? Well, I'm trying to talk like northern folks. That way they don't laugh at me so much."

"Do Ah have to talk funny?"

"No, sweetheart," she assured.

We got on the bus going to her neighborhood. By the time we had walked to her house from the bus stop, the streets were shrouded in darkness. We climbed the stairs to her third-floor room. She fed me a sweet roll and a cup of milk and started to tuck me in her bed. "No, Mothah," I protested. "Ah'm a big boy now. Fix me a pallet on the flo'."

So she did and I slept there beside her bed.

The next morning I figured she'd take me somewhere exciting, like the zoo. When I asked her where we'd be going for the day, she forced a smile. "We'll have our fun Saturday. That's mah day off. The othah days, Ah've gotta work."

My face dropped. "What'll Ah do while you'ah workin'?"

"You'll have to stay heah. I've got some little books from the library for you to read. An' I'll fix

41

you a good lunch. Before you know it, I'll be home to fix supper, then we can play a game together.

"Can Ah go outside while you'ah at work?"

"No, Jimmie. I want you to stay right in this room. And don't go makin' any noise or you might upset the landlady."

Mother fluffed her hair and powdered her nose before the mirror. She picked up her purse and gave me a quick kiss. "Now, remember: stay in the room and don't make any noise. Bye, I gotta be goin' or I'll be late."

And with that she left me "home alone."

Air conditioning was unheard of in those days, and Mother didn't even have a fan. Nor did she have a radio.

All day Wednesday, Thursday and Friday, I stayed in her room alone. I thought those days would never end.

Friday evening, the first words I heard when she walked in the door, were, "We're goin' to the zoo tomorrow."

I jumped up and down and squealed. She laid a finger over her lips. "Shhhh. My landlady doesn't like noise." I kept my voice down, but the anticipation of going back to the zoo kept me awake a long time.

What a glorious Saturday we had, until we got back to Mother's room. We were eating supper when Mother said, "You look so sad, darlin'. Didn't you have a good time today?"

I bobbed my head and forced a grin. "Yes'um, Ah had a real good time. But Ah wanna go back to the farm now. Ah love you, Mothah, but Ah don't lack havin' to stay shut up all day heah by mahsef."

Big tears welled up in her eyes and coursed down her rouged cheeks. "I wish I didn't have to leave you by yourself, Jimmie. I asked my boss if I could bring you with me to work, but he said you'd just be in the way."

I started begging. "Mothah., why can't yuh go back an' stay in Mississippi with me? If yuh cain't get a job in Hickory, yuh can hep Daddy Floyd on the farm."

"Son, this is Depression time. There aren't many jobs to be had. I've gotta stick with what I've got."

I don't remember all that we talked about that Saturday evening. I just know that she finally conceded I would be better off spending all my time on the farm. She got word to Daddy Floyd and Grandmother on the time to meet me at Meridian. They were there with bells on when my train pulled into the station and I ripped off the sign, "IN CARE OF THE CONDUCTOR."

That summer I learned to ride a hog. Daddy Floyd laughed loud enough to be heard all the way to Uncle Ban's pasture when he saw me cavorting in the hog lot. "Ride 'em hawgboy," he hollered, and I responded, "Wahoo! Wahoo!"

"Jennie has gotta see this," he chuckled and headed for the house to get Grandmother. She was not as amused as Daddy Floyd. Doris thought I was stupid. "Yuh smell like a hog, too," she said.

But Daddy Floyd loved my new skill. "Isn't Ruth's boy's sumthin'," my grandfather kept saying. "He might be a rodeo star one day."

Finally, though, Daddy Floyd began having second thoughts. "Boy, you'ah ridin' awl the fat off the hawgs," he said.

I kept telling myself I would stop after just one more romp around the pasture.

I had a special place where I jumped on a hog's back for a ride. A board fence separated the barn lot from the hog pasture. The hogs squirmed under the fence at a place where the bottom slat was broken out. Rain water turned this depression into slushy, stinky mud. With corn ears protruding from my hip pockets, I mounted the fence and spread my legs so a hog that came rooting through the muddy breach would have to pass between my legs. I'd bend over, holding an ear behind me, calling, "Heah, pig, heah, pig, sook, sook, sook."

I was perched there one warm afternoon when a big sow came oink-oink-oinking toward the hole in the fence. I dropped an ear to the ground. When the sow squeezed under the fence to get the corn, I dropped on her back. She tore out bucking and squealing across the pasture with me riding backward and cranking her tail.

She rounded a cluster of bushes, shook her back and dumped me on to the grass. I bounced and rolled to a stop and ran back to the fence to drop on another hog.

My hog busting career came to an abrupt end one day in August when I mounted a young boar that

Daddy Flood was raising for a breeder. He was smaller than the sows I usually rode but he looked tough and fast.

Facing the barn lot, I positioned myself on the fence and held the ear of corn behind me. "Heah, pig, heah pig, sook, sook, sook." He came rooting through the hole under the fence — oink, oink, oink — to get the corn. The instant I dropped on his back I knew I had a hog of another speed. That boar forgot all about the ear of corn and took off like a scalded dog across the pasture. I grabbed his tail and clamped my legs firmly around his back and belly to prepare for a long and rough ride. Suddenly he bolted to a stop, whirled around and dashed back toward the hole under the fence. I didn't have sense enough to roll off in time. The back of my head hit the second slat as the boar dived under.

There I lay face down in the soft mud, my head pounding with pain. With stinky hog droppings and gooey mud covering my face and chest, I jumped up and ran screaming toward the house for Grandmother. She and Aunt Lizzie cleaned me up while Doris stood by holding her nose, hollering, "Stinky! Stinky! Stinky!" I never had the slightest desire to ride a hog again the rest of my life.

That didn't mean I was ready to pay attention to Daddy Floyd and Grandmother. I had another lesson to learn.

It was hog farrowing time, when the sows gave birth to their pigs. A time when any hog farmer knows some animals can be dangerous. Most sows were eager to show off their brood, but now and then one would turn downright mean. Daddy Floyd had such a sow and warned me proper.

"Jimmie, keep out of the hog pasture until the sows bring up theah pigs. Yuh undahstand me, boy? That ole Beulah is actin' mean an' if she bit yuh an' tasted blood she'd jus' go on an' eat yuh up."

I had every intention of heeding Daddy Floyd's warning until one day I heard squealing that simply demanded an investigation. Climbing the fence, I cautiously approached the thick part of the pasture where the sows had beaten down the brush and weeds to make their birthing beds.

By this time I was getting scared. I decided to take one more turn in the path and go back. I eased forward and heard a rustle and a "Whuufh." There was Beulah and she was mad!

I whirled and bolted back toward the fence as fast as my thin legs could carry me. Being lighter, I could take the turns in the brush path more quickly than the big sow, which kept crashing into the brush. Finally I reached the end of the path and raced into the open part of the hog pasture. I was about thirty feet ahead of Beulah, but she was fast gaining on me in the open ground.

She stayed right on my bare heels as I ran parallel to the small stream that coursed its way down the middle of the pasture. At the last possible second I veered left, leaped across the little rivulet and dashed toward the safety of the fence some fifty feet away.

Crossing the stream slowed Beulah just barely enough. As I dived over the fence, I heard a vicious pop as Beulah crashed against the fence behind me.

I backed up to watch as she hurled herself furiously at the fence again and again.

Fearing she'd break through the fence, I retreated out of her sight into the corn field. I worked my way back to the house and climbed up the chinaberry tree in the back yard so I could see over the corn stalks. There she was, grunting in anger and pacing back and forth.

My heart was running a mile a minute. "Thank yuh, Jesus. Oh, thank yuh, Jesus," I mouthed over and over. "From now on, Ah'm gonna listen tuh Daddy Floyd."

After a while I slid down the tree and tiptoed into the house. Aunt Lizzie was peeling potatoes. Grandmother was in the parlor patching a shirt. Doris looked up and saw me, my face still red from the chase. "Well, Jimmie," she said, "what trouble have yuh been in this time?"

I glared at Doris. "Ah outrun ole Beulah."

"That ole sow was chasin' you?" Aunt Lizzie said.

"Yep, and she couldn't catch me."

"Jimmie?" Grandmother called. "A lettah came from youah Mothah."

She handed me the piece of mail.

A big grin spread over my face. "I hope you're having a good time back on the farm," she said. "I'll be down to see you as soon as the boss gives me a few days off.

"I wish you could come and see me, but I'm just not able to care for you now. Maybe next year will be better."

47

In Care of the Conductor

I handed the letter back to Grandmother and asked, "How long till dinnah? Ah'm stahved."

Chapter 5

" 'Hey-Maude' and Doris"

Grandmother saw the headline about the child of America's flying hero and snatched up the **Meridian Star**.

LINDBERGH BABY KIDNAPPED!

"Oh, Lord," she moaned, "what's gonna happen next?"

The story stayed on the front page. Six weeks later they found the child — dead!

I had nightmares. Boy did I have nightmares. One of the worst ones came after Mother left me on the farm and returned to St. Louis.

A big masked man was trying to tear me limb from limb. Cecil and Vernell were sawing logs in the bed next to me, oblivious to my fright.

I finally crept out of the room and knocked lightly on the door of the girls' bedroom. Aunt Helen Maude, six years older than I, quietly opened the door and held me until my heart stopped pounding like a jack hammer. Then to keep me from disturbing Doris, my older aunt let me fall asleep beside her. When the first light of day seeped into the room, she sent me quickly back to my bed so nobody else would ever know I had been so scared.

I don't know how many times Helen Maude rescued me from night demons. That first year without Mother, she was my guardian angel. I called her by my own boyish contraction, "Hey-Maude," which she didn't seem to resent.

Dear Hey-Maude's skin was angelic white. Like many Southern young women of her day, she worked very hard to stay out of the sun.

A sun tan marked a girl as a "field hand." Hey-Maude let her blonde hair grow down to her shoulders every year. Then she'd bring out the scissors and say, "Ah've gotta get this hot stuff off mah neck."

Aunt Hey-Maude suffered because of my constant provocations of Aunt Doris, only a year and four days my senior. Once when I was mad at Doris, I ran ahead of both aunts when we were walking along the road toward the house.

The girls didn't know I had discovered a yellow jacket nest in the ditch that ran along the right side of the road. Grabbing up a stick, I "jobbed" it up and down, stirring the fiery creatures to a frenzy. I left the stick in the hole so the jackets couldn't get out and ran back past Doris and Hey-Maude to trail behind them.

Just as the two came abreast of the nest, I came racing past them with a full head of steam, cackling like a mad rooster, leaning over to jerk the stick out of the hole. Instantly, my aunts saw the clever thing I'd done and they started running too. Doris shot past me first, her long, skinny legs pumping like a steam locomotive's drivers, screeching, "Jimmie Rogers, Ah'm gonna kill yuh!"

Hey-Maude passed me too! And I didn't even know she could run.

All at once the situation changed very dramatically and I was first in line for the yellow jackets' feast! I quit squandering energy in cackling and diverted it to something more important. Like out-running the angry yellow jackets.

Well, nobody got stung, so it should have ended as a clever prank right there. But no, Doris just had to tell on me and Grandmother made me apologize to them. Oh, puke!

Hey-Maude looked like she felt sorry for me, but Doris stood back grinning from behind Grandmother's skirt. There was nothing I could do except grind my teeth and say the painful words. Later I wrapped my arms around Hey-Maude and told her how badly I felt about almost getting her stung. I figured the forced apology was all Doris deserved.

I practically worshiped Hey-Maude and she spoiled me like a baby. I don't think either of us spoke sharply to the other during all our years together on the farm. Doris, tall and angular but blonde like my mother, was in my childish mind, a brat and a snot. And I'm sure that the feeling was mutual about me.

Take the time Doris and I were examining an old rusty Model T that had been left by its owner just off the road. "Look an' see if theah's any gas left in the tank," I urged. "If theah is, we might take a ride."

Both Daddy Floyd and Grandmother had told us to never, never strike a match close to gasoline. I was the type who had to test out everything. This time, I decided to let Doris do it.

Doris was already peering down the dark fillerneck. "Jimmie, Ah can't see a thing."

I dug a match from a pocket in my cutoffs and handed it to her. "Heah, use a light, dummy."

She raked the match head across the rusty fender. Vroom! A column of fire shot up and enveloped her face. I instantly feared that she'd been hurt — badly.

Her eye lashes, top and bottom, her eyebrows and the front part of her hair were just gone! All I could see was a white face sticking out of a frizzly bush of hair.

She saw me staring goggle-eyed and she felt her face. Then she started running for the house, hollering, "Jimmie Rogers, Ah'm gonna kill yuh!"

Although Doris didn't appear to be scarred, Grandmother was not amused. "Apologize, Jimmie. Tell her you'ah sorry. Yuh could have killed her."

I looked at her face, absent of eyebrows. "Ah'm sorry," I whispered and started giggling.

"Tell her again," Grandmother demanded.

I just couldn't stop giggling. Finally, Grandmother told Doris to turn her back. "Now say it again, Jimmie."

I did — this time, without giggling.

Doris and I weren't constantly trying to outdo one another. I think she saw me as her understudy, and sometimes her slave. At times I had to concede that she really cared for me.

Like when she saved me from having to repeat a grade in Hickory.

On the first day of school Doris trailed along behind Grandmother when she went to introduce me to Miss Haley, who taught both the second and third grades at Hickory. She tested me on reading and writing. I missed a number of words and could only print letters. The teacher shook her head sadly at Grandmother. "Miz Jennie, Ah don't think he's ready foah the next grade."

Doris' facial hair had grown back to normal. Having been promoted to the third grade, she had been standing in back of Grandmother listening.

"Miz Haley," Doris proposed, "Ah'll hep Jimmie keep up. Put me on the right side of the third grade bunch, next to him. Ah'll hep him when he needs it."

The teacher threw Doris a bright smile. "That's sweet of yuh to want to help you'ah little brothah."

"Oh, Miz Haley, don't yuh know? He's only my nephew."

Despite her offer to help, I could have crowned her for that.

We sat at old-fashioned desks with ornate cast iron legs. The hard maple top sported pencil grooves and an inkwell hole near the right upper edge. Doris turned out to be one of the best teachers I ever had. At school and at home, stretched on the braided rag rug in Grandmother's bedroom, my young aunt taught me to "sound out" syllables for recitation. She listened to me read. She corrected my spelling. She quizzed me on geography. With Doris as my instructor, I came to look forward to the weekly spelling bees and geography "stand downs" at Hickory School.

We didn't have illegal drugs, sex education, early pregnancies, values destruction, put downs of "old-fashioned" parents, or guns in Hickory School. There was not one "functional illiterate," either.

We brought our own lunch composed of thick country bacon, fried eggs tucked in Grandmother's biscuits, plus cornbread, onions and buttermilk — all stuffed into an old lard can. The teachers swept the floors with the help of the students and once a week we all pitched in to wash the windows and the blackboards. Our principal also taught three classes a day. If somebody had proposed the idea of a superintendent, they would have been laughed out of Newton County.

Before and after school Doris and I had chores at home. We hoed the garden, picked vegetables, shelled beans and peas, dried dishes and beat the clothes on wash day after they had been boiled in the wash pot with shaved yellow bar soap. My favorite job was chopping and stacking stovewood, then bringing in an armful at Grandmother's request. Down the corridors of time even now I can hear her calling:

Stove wood Jack, stove wood Jack,
You oughta be theah an' ha'fway back.

Not having plumbing, we used the outhouse during the day. When nature called at night, there was the slop jar, known in St. Louis as the chamber pot. My first fight of the day with Doris usually came over the question of, "who emptied the slop jar yestahday?"

The fussin' started when Grandmother discovered the jar hadn't been taken out that morning. "Who emptied the jar yestuhday?"

"Ah did," I insisted.

"Jimmie's lyin'," Doris countered. "Ah emptied that stinky jar."

Grandmother's eyes swept over us. "One of yuh has got a mighty poah memory."

"Grandmother, I remembah emptyin' the jar," I solemnly declared.

Doris threw me a scorching glare. "Jimmie remembahs what he wants to remembah."

In the end Grandmother arbitrated and one of us walked out grumbling to the field, past our back yard, holding the slop jar at arm's length in one hand, gripping our nose with the other. The corn always grew greenest and highest near the James sewage disposal plot.

Shrewd Doris had a knack for getting her way with me. Sometimes I caught on and rebelled. Other times I bargained with her to get what was important to me.

On this warm Saturday in March I got a real bad itch to try my luck fishing in Chunky River. Hey-Maude was visiting with a girl friend. Cecil and Vernell were still working away from home. I looked over at my blonde nemesis. "Doris, Ah heah the fish ah really bitin' in ole Chunky."

She threw me a "who cares"? look.

"Ah'll empty the slop jar three mawnin's in a row if you'll go fishin' with me," I offered.

I could see that wasn't enough. I was just about to up the slop jar days to five, when her eyes squinched down to little slits and a sly, cunning look spread over her face. I should have taken warning but I rushed in like a sheep eager for a trimming.

"Do yuh really want me t'go fishin' with yuh, Jimmie?" she asked in that, oh, so innocent voice.

"Ah sho do," I quickly answered.

"Well, if yuh want me t'do somethin' foah yuh, then you'll hafta do somethin' foah me," she cajoled softly.

Suddenly on guard, I asked, "Like what?"

"Well, if you'd play papah dolls with me this mawnin', Ah'd go fishin' with yuh in the aftahnoon," she bargained.

I thought fast. On the one hand I didn't want to play paper dolls like a sissy but on the other I didn't want to fish alone. "Would anybody hafta know?" I asked, naively trying to strike a bargain—but way over my head against her artifice.

Doris assured me in her syrupy voice, "Why no, Jimmie. Co'se not. Nobody in the whole wide world would hafta know."

And so the bargain was made, a contract I'd later regret. It wasn't enough that I had to cut out the dolls dressed in their underwear and then dress them. Doris made me do loathsome things like pretending to be a girl and talking in a high pitched voice, saying odious words like "Kitchy Koo" and "Babykins."

Finally, the disgusting morning was over. After dinner I dug a can of worms. Carrying our fishing poles, we took a shortcut across Uncle Ban's south field to reach a special fishing hole. But to do so we had to contend with Brutus, Uncle Ban's big black bull.

All the way over to the pasture I kept trying to tell Doris about my clever ways of outwitting Brutus. A couple of times I had to ask, "Ah you listenin'?" because it looked as if her mind was wandering.

"Quit bein' silly? Of co'se Ah'm listenin'." That was her standard response to me: "Quit bein' silly."

We reached the pasture fence and I quickly spotted Brutus. He was about fifty yards out with his head turned away from us. Quietly we slipped through the barbed wire, making sure our poles didn't hit the wire, and started walking through the grass.

I was watching Brutus out of the corner of my eye, when he raised his head and saw us! He looked us over for a few seconds, then started in our direction. I speeded up a little to keep the same distance between the bull and myself but that stupid Doris just kept moping along.

"Hurry up Doris, he's gainin' on you!" But she didn't seem a bit concerned, even when Brutus began dashing toward her. "Run, Doris, run!" I shouted, throwing all caution to the wind and racing toward the far fence.

That stupid girl still didn't see the danger and just kept strolling along. Reaching the safety of the fence I turned to watch the scene, fearful that she would get gored.

I kept hoping she would run but at the last minute when it became obvious she wouldn't, I dashed toward Brutus to distract him. He whirled and started after me, giving Doris time to amble to the fence and ease between the barbed wires. I had to dive under the bottom strand to escape the bull's sharp horns.

To make matters worse, Doris caught the biggest fish. Nevertheless, I made sure that Brutus was far from us when we walked home because I wasn't sure I'd distract him a second time.

She kept trying to talk to me, but each time I said, "Aw, jus' shut up, Doris!" All in all it was a thoroughly miserable afternoon.

That night at the supper table I kept waiting for her to say something about how I almost got butted by the bull. I also expected her to brag about catching the biggest fish but she didn't mention that either.

Not until the next Saturday, over in Hickory, did I discover what she'd been plotting. My friends and I were in Chapman's Drug Store having a soda pop and enjoying the big pedestal fan when Doris, Dell Brand and Katherine Ann Knight entered. As they passed our table Doris stopped just long enough to say sweetly, "Jimmie, did yuh tell yoah fri'n's 'bout playin' papah dolls with me?"

I choked on my Nehi grape soda and could have dropped straight through the floor. No chance of trying to deny it though, because my face turned blood red and told the whole story. I mumbled something about humoring her because she had been saying some crazy things ever since Daddy Floyd's mule kicked her in the head. But my friends didn't hear me because they were laughing too hard. I tried to get them to shut up so maybe I could recover a tiny shred of self-respect but they wouldn't. In the end I stomped barefooted out of the drug store and crossed the street to the park. I was so mad at Doris I could just spit and I kicked a big, dry clod of dirt as hard as I could. I almost split my big toe open.

I figured if it hadn't been for Doris I wouldn't have gotten so mad and hurt myself. I spent the next fifteen minutes devising hideous tortures involving ant hills, yellow jacket nests and bull whips. I watched from the park as she walked out of the drug store and went to wait in the car for Daddy Floyd. Limping over to the car I started berating her but she just smiled sweet-like and said, "Why Jimmie, what on earth happened to you'ah foot?"

"Yuh jus' don't worry none 'bout my foot. It was all you'ah fault anyhow," I retorted.

She looked surprised and that made me even madder. I ranted and raved at her, almost out of control. "Yuh told! Yuh told! An' yuh promised yuh wouldn't. Yuh lied 'bout not tellin' anybody 'bout me playin' papah dolls with yuh. Yuh planned it all along."

She painted her face with an innocent look and answered piously, "No, Ah didn't lie, Jimmie, Ah jus' said they didn't hafta know. An' they didn't—Ah jus' chose to tell 'um." I clenched up my fists as hard as I could to keep from choking her. In that instant I thought God would have surely forgiven me for doing her harm.

I learned to spell out conditions in the most meticulous detail in any contract I made with Doris after that. When somebody mentioned her name, I remarked, "Oh, are yuh talkin' about Doris the Snot?"

Doris, of course, had a few choice adjectives for me. "Dumb" and "Stupid" were two of her favorites.

Years later I came to understand that we were merely caught up in sibling rivalry. By kinship we were aunt and nephew. In function we were brother and sister.

And "Hey-Maude" was my beloved big sister.

Chapter 6

"The Rumor"

We were gathered around the fireplace in my grandparents' bedroom on a cold December evening in 1933. Doris and I lay stretched across the rug doing our homework on a history lesson about the great World War of fourteen years past.

Daddy Floyd burst through the door with an armful of wood. As he was beefing up the fire, a question came that had been bothering me all evening. I figured if anybody knew the answer, Daddy Floyd would.

"How do ya keep a war from startin'?" I asked.

Daddy Floyd pushed in another log. I repeated my question.

Daddy Floyd straightened and turned to look at me. "I heard yuh the first time, Jimmie. I'm tryin' to think of an answer."

Grandmother spoke up. "Floyd, tell them about the time yuh kept white fokes an' black fokes from fightin' in the Chunky Swamp."

Daddy Floyd shook the loose dirt off his overalls into the fire.

"Tell them, Floyd," she persisted.

"We want to know," Doris chimed in.

It took a lot more urging to get Daddy Floyd talking about the time when he prevented a probable race war. I didn't get it all that night. In fact it was several years before I got all the information from Daddy Floyd for the story that appears here. I've written it in the third person since it happened five years before I was born. The attempt at literary flair is mine.

The mule-drawn wagon creaked down the line of murky shapes, most of them standing halfway off the road and some all the way in the ditch. The acrid odor of man and mule sweat permeated the sticky-hot air of that June night in 1919. Mules shuffled and swished their tails at imagined flies but little else broke the silence of the fearful. The wind-sown clouds thinned occasionally and faintly revealed for the briefest of moments white-eyed men and older boys on the seats of wagons, or standing at a skittish mule's head holding its bridle.

More was sensed than seen as the men and boys waited for some action. Faint moonlight broke through a thin section of clouds, furtively glinting on shotguns, pitch forks and axes. Fear lurked in the hearts of these men on the red clay road that approached the bridge from the south at the edge of the Chunky River swamp. Fear of the night. Dread of what men of another color might do before morning.

The latecomer pulled his mules to a halt at the head of the ghostly line.

"Floyd James? Floyd? Is that you?" inquired an anxious voice from the darkness.

"Yeah, it's me — and mah two sons, Cecil and Vernell. Is that you, Luthah? Who else is heah?"

Luther spoke in a hoarse, ragged whisper. "Yeah, it's me, an' mah two brothahs an' theah sons an' jus' 'bout all the men from Sixteenth Church. Lots of other fokes too. Maybe a hundahd uv us all told."

"How the Sam Hill, Luthah, did this crazy thing get goin'?" Daddy Floyd asked. "Ah jus' heard that white fokes an' black fokes were about to go to war at the Chunky bridge. Ah came as soon as Ah could get heah."

"Floyd, Ah jus' don't know all the particulars. A rider come up to mah place and he — Ah don't even know who he was — an' said he'd heard the nigras were on a rampage an' goin' to murdah a bunch of white fokes. Told me the white men were meetin' at the Harris place to head the nigras off as they come out of the swamp at the Chunky bridge."

Daddy Floyd blew through his lips, making a slight whooo sound. "Good Lawd! All this because of a rumah! If one of yuh fokes gets trigger itchy an' fires a shot, lots of people could get killed."

The respected man who would later become my grandfather took command. "Pass the word, Luthah foah evahbody to unload theah shotguns an' rifles. Tell them Ah requested it. They can keep the guns *open with shells in theah hand, but foah God's sake don't anybody shoot until Ah say so."*

Luther slipped into the darkness and whispers floated on the night air, as Daddy Floyd's request passed down the length of wagons and buggies. Luther soon returned to the Floyd wagon.

"Luthah, tell me what the situation is. Wheah ah the nigras?"

"Jus' across the Chunky River bridge, Floyd. We've got people behind them on the road — maybe twenty men. And we've got men with rifles in the trees down in the swamp. Won't none of them nigras get away if shootin' stahts."

Daddy Floyd shivered at the offhand talk of killing. He drew his coat tighter, buttoning it. The fear of a bloody race war made his blood run cold, even on this warm night.

"Has anybody talked to any of the nigras, Luthah? Do yuh know they'ah really theah?"

"No, nobody's talked to them, but we know they'ah theah. Clyde Harrison crawled down to the bridge an' said he could heah leather harness creakin' — and some whispahin' too. What are yuh gonna do, Floyd?"

"Well, Ah reckon Ah'll jus' go on over an' talk to them."

"Talk to the nigras? Floyd, yuh don't wanna do that. They'll cut you down like a mad dawg!"

"Luthah, Ah know all the nigras aroun' heah. They know whut Ah stand foah. Ah don't want to get

hurt, but if Ah don't talk to them while it's still dark, theah's goin' to be lots of fokes shot at daylight when people staht seein' movement."

Daddy Floyd handed the reins to his son, Vernell, and climbed down from the wagon seat to the marshy ground. Reaching up, he passed over his shotgun to his older son, Cecil, saying, "Yuh boys stay calm. Yuh heah me, now?"

"Yessuh, Papa, we'll be all right. Don't you worry none bout us," answered his thirteen-year-old firstborn.

Vernell, five years younger, added in a trembly voice, "Papa, yuh be careful. Them nigras won't be able to tell yuh from any othah white man in the dark."

Daddy Floyd walked down the middle of the road toward the bridge a hundred yards away with more than a little anxiety. The incongruous scent of magnolia blossoms tempered the tannic acid smell of the swamp. Reaching the bridge he stopped and cupped a hand behind each ear. He heard only the gurgling of the water as it flowed over a log.

"Hallo," he called in a strong voice. "Is anybody theah?"

Silence.

"Hallo. This heah is Floyd James. Ah'd like to talk to yuh."

This time a voice answered from just across the bridge. The nearness startled my grandfather.

"Is yuh white folks gon' kill us awl, Mistuh James? We ain't done nuthin' to nobody."

The voice sounded familiar.

"Is that yuh, Sylvester?"

"Yassuh, it's me, Sylvester Monroe."

"Walk this way," Daddy Floyd requested, *"an' Ah'll come tow'd yuh."*

Both men moved nearer so they could better be heard.

"Sylvester, will yuh tell me whut in the name of heaven is goin' on. Why ah awl yuh fokes ganged up an' goin' aroun' ahmed?"

"We wuz told yuh white fokes wuz gon' kill us in our sleep, Mistuh James."

"Who told yuh a fool thing like that?"

"Two white boys in Hickory. Mistuhes John Forsyth an' Mistuh Rube Young. We' ah jus heah to protect ouhseves. 'Pears to me we got good reason. Elsewise, why is a big crowd of white fokes waitin' foah us with guns on the othah side of the bridge?"

Daddy Floyd chuckled slightly under his breath, but Sylvester heard.

"Whut yuh laughin' 'bout, Mistuh James?"

" 'Cause Ah got the feelin' we white fokes have been made fools of too, Sylvester. Them white boys that told yuh that story were prob'ly the same ones that spread the rumah that nigras were goin' to shoot some white men."

"You sho of that, Mister Floyd?"

"Co'se Ah'm sho. Luthah Hampton wouldn't lie to me."

"Ah b'leve's yuh, Mistuh Floyd. Ah've allus b'leved in you. Ah tells black people, 'If yuh can't trust Mistuh Floyd James, hain't no white man yuh kin trust."

"An' Ah believe in yuh, Sylvester. Now let's get this thing stopped 'fo somebody does somethin' crazy. Walk back to youah end uv the bridge an' call three of yoah people to come up on the bridge unha'med and Ah'll call up three of mine. Have youah men bring a lantern, but don't let it be lit."

"Yassuh, Mistuh Floyd. Ah agrees with that. Ah'll get mah three."

Floyd strode back to the other end of the bridge and cupped his hands to his mouth. "Luthah! Come up heah on the bridge and bring Vernon and Clyde. Leave youah shotguns behind, but bring an unlit lantern."

Luther's voice came floating across the water. "Floyd, we ain't gonna walk into no trap."

"Luthah, if yuh get shot, I get shot. I'm tellin' yuh that both races have been made fools of by two lunatic white boys who could have gotten some of us killed. Now come on up. Yuh heah?"

The peace delegations came from either end of the bridge and met with Floyd James.

Daddy Floyd positioned himself between Luther and Sylvester. "Who told yuh some whites were out to kill some of youah?" he asked Sylvester.

"Two white boys, Mistuhes John Forsyth an' Rube Young."

Daddy Floyd turned to his friend and fellow church member, Luther. "Who spread the story that some black folks were gunning foah white men?"

"Same two boys, Ah spec. They oughta be tah'd an' feat' had"

"Now that yuh understand one another," Daddy Floyd said, "let's light the lanterns. Truth flows better when we can look each othah in the eye."

While the men talked, night faded quietly into morning. Off in the east, above Meridian, strands of orange light laced the sky. They shook hands, then retraced their steps to carry the message of peace back to their companions.

No blood was spilled.

Daddy Floyd climbed into his wagon and awoke his sleeping sons. "It's awl ovah," he said. "Theah won't be any shootin'."

Thus assured, Cecil leaned his head against his father's shoulder in sleep and Vernell's chin tilted down to Daddy Floyd's chest. Up from the swamp the dense fog rolled, pushing cool air before it. Daddy Floyd smiled to himself. "It's goin' to be a long day plowing. Maybe Ah oughta let the boys stay abed an' come out in the fields later." He reached his arms about his sons and drew them closer to his warmth.

I came along as Floyd James' grandson five years later. As the years passed, various versions of what happened that night circulated around Newton County. One version spoke of "The Battle of Chunky River" and claimed that a large number of men had been killed, both white and black. Another account said thousands had been involved. Neither variant had all the facts straight. The story I've told here is the true account of how two meddlesome farm boys almost started a war, and how my grandfather, Benjamin Floyd James nipped the threat in the bud.

Daddy Floyd, of course, didn't make himself out to be a hero. "I jus' did what any Christian man oughta do," he said. "Theah's no need of people fightin' when they can talk."

Chapter 7

"Daddy Floyd: My Guiding Star"

Benjamin Floyd James stood an even six feet tall, towering over me like a giant. His arms swung loosely at his sides as he took long purposeful strides. The muscles in his upper arms bulged out like rounded rocks from years of blacksmithing. His clear, blue-grey eyes, set under a full thatch of light, sandy hair were usually kind, but could quickly turn granite when he felt himself or one of his loved ones threatened. When he became angry, really angry, his voice dropped to a whisper and people got out of his way. He never whispered at me.

"Daddy" Floyd was born December 18, 1881, one of ten children. He was my grandfather and my role model. I adored him.

Daddy Floyd's father witnessed General William T. Sherman's shameful march of destruction across Newton County and Thaddeus Stevens' ill-famed rule of "Reconstruction." Stevens' ruthless carpetbaggers reduced Mississippi from fifth among the states in per capita wealth, in 1861, to dead last in 1877. Three years later, northern timber companies carted off entire stands of virgin pines, despoiling much of the land in the county.

Daddy Floyd's family never owned a single slave. Yet they suffered privation and poverty that would take almost a century for them to overcome.

In 1902 Daddy Floyd married Jennie Mabel Armstrong — my grandmother. They scraped together enough money to buy a section of 640 acres that spread across a low rolling plain between the Chunky River and the Okahatta Creek swamps. These were not swamps in the classic sense, but merely low lying areas that flooded easily. As Uncle Ban Allen used to say, "All yuh gotta do is spit an' yuh got a flood."

Daddy Floyd cut and hauled timber to the Hickory saw mill. From the lumber he constructed the sprawling French style farm home that I came to love. He built the house with a big front porch facing west, so the prevailing breeze would sweep down the wide, high-ceilinged, 40-foot long and 12-foot wide hallway to the dining room. The smallest bedroom leading off the hallway was 20 by 22 feet and easily accommodated two double beds with plenty of room for other furniture. Insulation of pine sheeting made our residence the coolest house in the area in summer and the warmest in winter.

Whatever Daddy Floyd did, he did well. Besides his skills in farming and carpentry, he was a master butcher, blacksmith, wagon maker, shoemaker, broom maker, cabinet craftsman and toy maker for his children and red-headed grandson (me!).

Just to watch him work was a real pleasure. He matched grains of wood almost perfectly, going over piece after piece of lumber to find the perfect correspondence, even if the finished product was to be painted. I asked him once why it was so important to match boards so carefully when they would be painted over.

He flashed a quick response. "Wael, Jimmie, it would be jus' as strong an' be covahd by paint, but evah time Ah looked at it Ah'd know Ah hadden done my best."

He took pride in his crops. He competed with other farmers to get the first bale of cotton to the gin and win a bonus. When he won, as he frequently did, he brought us all special presents from town.

Daddy Floyd was also a Baptist deacon who believed God-fearing people should involve themselves in politics. "If politics is dirty," he said, "it's 'cause not enough Christians do theah duty." He ran for tax assessor and road supervisor, but was defeated both times by better known town candidates from Hickory. After the second loss, he commended the winner and said, "Maybe the Lawd jus' wants me t'do farmin'."

Daddy Floyd despised government handouts. One day on a trip into Hickory we passed the Bill Woods place. Mr. Woods was out in his cotton field plowing up his cotton plants. Surprised, I asked Daddy Floyd, "Why is he doin' that?"

"The guv'ment pays him to do it."

I was flabbergasted. "Why wud they pay him to plow up his cotton?"

"So theah'll be less cotton on the mahket an' Mr. Woods will get a highah price foah the rest of his cotton." He looked across at me. "What do yuh think of that, Jimmie?"

"If Mr. Woods can get the money from the guv'ment, why shudden he take it?" I answered, feeling a bit uneasy.

"Now jus' think, Jimmie. Wheah do you think the guv'ment gets its money."

"Ah don't rightly know. Taxes?"

"That's right, son. Now answer me this. S'pose Mr. Woods was to run out heah on the road an' wave me to a stop. S'pose he stuck a gun in mah ribs an' said, 'Give me three hundred dollahs 'cause Ah'm not gettin' enough money foah my cotton.' What would yuh think of that?"

My face flamed in indignation. "That's jus' not right! That'd be robbin'."

"Then why is it right foah him to go to the guv'ment an' get them to pass a law that let's him have mah tax dollahs without him havin' to use a gun?"

I saw the wrongness of the system. "Can't somebody do somethin'?"

"Don't worry," Daddy Floyd said confidently. "City folks will put a stop to this right soon. President Roosevelt stahted this giveaway an' it won't last long." Later he admitted, "Ah've been proven wrong. City folks want guv'ment money too."

While Daddy Floyd didn't like government handouts, he believed in helping people, white and black, who wanted to work.

Oliver Jenkins, the husband of our beloved "Aunt" Lizzie, was one of his sharecroppers. One day he timidly approached Daddy Floyd in the farm shop.

"Mistuh Floyd, uh, uh, kin Ah speak with yuh a minute."

Daddy Floyd raised up from his blacksmith forge. "What's on yuh mind, Olivah?"

"Mistah Floyd, Ah bin happy farmin' wif yuh."

"And Ah've been happy with yuh an' Lizzie," Daddy Floyd said, wondering what Oliver was getting at.

Oliver looked down at the dirt floor. "Mistuh Floyd, would it hurt youah feelins', if Ah said, Ah wonts ta buy a fahm fo muh ownself. Ain't many black folks own their own place, Mistuh Floyd."

"That's true, Olivah. Some white folks don't want 'um too. Me, Ah'm all for a man, any man havin' his own property."

Oliver grinned. "I thought you'd see it that way, Mistuh Floyd."

Daddy Floyd squinted at Oliver. "I'd sho hate to lose yuh, but if yuh can make it on yuh own, then Ah'm not gonna stand in youah way."

"Yassuh, that's whut Ah'd lack ta do."

"Yuh got the money, I reckon," Daddy Floyd said.

"Nawsuh, Ah ain't, but Ah thinks Ah kin borrah it from the bank in Hickory. The banker theah, he knows me and Lizzie ah good, honest black fokes. Ah b'lieve he'll loan me whut it takes ta buy the place Lizzie an' me got our eyes on."

A couple of weeks later Oliver came back to my grandfather. His head drooped.

"Mistuh Floyd, the Hickory banker turned me down. I went to some other bankers in the county and they all said no. I guess Ah'll jus hafta keep on sharecroppin'."

Daddy Floyd touched his black friend on the shoulder. "Oliver, how much yuh need?"

Oliver named the amount, adding, "Ah don't want a real big farm. Ah jus want a little land Ah kin call mah own."

"Let me see what Ah can do," Daddy Floyd said.

A couple of days later Daddy Floyd rode into town and mortgaged his own farm to get the money his sharecropper needed. He walked out to the shop where Oliver was shoeing a horse.

"Yuh still wanna buy youah own place, Olivah?" Daddy Floyd asked.

Oliver looked up. "Wuz than anything in the world, Mistuh Floyd, but I done give up aftah them banks turnt me down."

"What would yuh think if Ah was to loan yuh the money?"

Oliver couldn't believe what he had heard. "Say that ag'in, Mistuh Floyd. Say it real slow."

Daddy Floyd repeated the question.

Oliver reached up and grasped Daddy Floyd's hand. "Oh, Mistuh Floyd, me and Lizzie would be foevah thankful. We'd make a big payment evah time we took cotton to the gin."

"We got a deal," Daddy Floyd said. "Go to youah house an' get cleaned up an' we'll go into Hickory an' sign the papers."

Oliver paid back every cent. However, some white folks weren't happy when they heard about Daddy Floyd helping his black sharecropper get his own farm. "Yuh give a nigra an inch an' he'll take a mile," they said. "God didn't mean foah nigra's to own property."

Daddy Floyd didn't believe that way at all. "Jimmie," he told me one day, "evah man's as good as anothuh in the Lawd's sight. Evah man oughta have the chance to improve his state of livin'."

Daddy Floyd was also my sex education teacher. When I was about ten he took me with him across Okahatta Creek to breed a heifer with Carl Brown's bull. Leading the young cow I walked alongside my grandfather as we crossed through the swamp and creek. As we neared the Brown barn, the bull bellowed fiercely and the heifer became very nervous.

"What's wrong with them?" I asked Daddy Floyd.

"They've got the urge to mate," he said with a sly grin.

Daddy Floyd turned the heifer loose in the barn lot and Mr. Brown let his bull out of the stall. It was a new sight to me and I had dozens of questions for Daddy Floyd. He answered them all calmly and explained the difference between animal urges and human love responses. "Theah's nothin' to be ashamed of," he said, "so long as you follow God's plan."

Daddy Floyd invested in a high bred stud horse and three mares. He let them run free in the pasture, but to keep them gentle he doled out a little grain when they came up to the barn. Almost every night they led the cows home for their feeding.

One windy morning the western sky clouded over. Around ten o'clock the air got dead still. The birds vanished. The chickens fled to their roosts. The still air hung oppressively and I felt the hair raise on the back of my neck.

From the porch I looked across the west fields and saw sheets of rain advancing toward us.

The cows came on to the barn but the stud and his mares stayed in the woods. By the next morning Oakhatta Creek and Chunky River were out of their banks and surging into the woods.

Vernell, thirteen years older than I, was home for awhile helping Daddy Floyd on the farm. "Looks lack the horses ahn't comin' home," Daddy Floyd said to him. "We'd best go drive them in foah the watah gets any highah."

I stepped up beside Daddy Floyd and my twenty-one-year-old uncle. "Ah'm goin' with yuh and 'Nell."

"Not this time, Jimmie," Daddy Floyd said. "The watah may already be over youah head in the swamps."

They marched bravely off in their oilskin raincoats and disappeared in the dark rain. All we could do was pray. Some three hours later, they came dragging back, splotched with mud. Daddy Floyd was crying.

"Did yuh rescue the horses?" Grandmother wanted to know.

Daddy Floyd sorrowfully shook his head.

"We found the stud an' mares standin' in watah above theah bellies," Vernell recounted. "We drove 'um out of the swamp, then they fell in a deep slough an' the mares got tangled in muscadine vines." He paused to give Daddy Floyd a chance to pick up the story. Daddy Floyd just stood there, staring at the floor. Grandmother stepped over and grasped his arm.

"The stud," Vernell continued, "tried to herd the mares out an' got caught in the vines. Ah slipped a rope 'round his neck, but cudden pull him free. Ah dove down an' tried to free the hosses' legs and got kicked in the head. If Daddy hadn't pulled me out, I'd a drowned theah foah sho."

Daddy Floyd nodded.

"We found a little high spot," Vernell said sadly, "an' stayed theah an' watched that cold muddy watah inch ovah the poah hosses heads."

Daddy Floyd choked back another sob as he broke in. "Those were good hosses. Ah jus' wish theah was some way we could uv saved 'um. All we could do was stay with 'um to the end."

For days after that Daddy Floyd was disconsolate. When his eyes teared up, Grandmother hugged him and talked very softly. He never tried raising horses again.

Daddy Floyd was giving to a fault, but he didn't believe in wasting money when he could save a dime. Sunday mornings, he hitched up the mules and we rode the four miles to church in a wagon. Gasoline for the car cost all of eight cents a gallon.

Daddy Floyd and Grandmother were members of Sixteenth Baptist Church, so named because the original land deed specified that one sixteenth of the original property must forever be set aside for a church house and cemetery.

Their beloved son, Lamar, cut down in 1919 by blood poisoning when he was only four, lay buried in Sixteenth Church's graveyard. Every Sunday when we attended services and every Wednesday night when we went to prayer meeting, Grandmother crossed the road to stand by his grave for a brief time. Daddy Floyd waited patiently and never intruded. He knew she needed this grief-time with Lamar.

We always arrived a few minutes before services began. Grandmother — after visiting Lamar's grave — followed Helen Maude and Doris into the church house to socialize with the women folks. Daddy Floyd took time to talk to the men about crops, the weather and world news in general. I stayed out in the churchyard to get in a fast game of tag or to show off a new toy Daddy Floyd had made for me.

At the proper time the men and boys trooped through the door. When I was small, I sat with Grandmother and my aunts on the "Sisters' side," of the church. Smelling of talcum powder, Grandmother sat erect, a straw hat perched on her head and wearing a lace-trimmed, floral dress. "Sit up straight lack a man," she told me.

It was a milestone when I was judged well-behaved and big enough to move to the Brothers' side. Daddy Floyd wore his high starched collar and seersucker suit and I sat next to him trying to justify his faith in me by not falling asleep.

It was easy to stay awake during the singing. Sister Emmaline stomped away energetically on the old foot-powered pump organ while the congregation sang, "In the Sweet By and By," "Rock of Ages" and other best-loved hymns. The booming voices of Daddy Floyd and the other men gave me the shivers. I sat in absolute awe when they launched into, "Give Me That Old Time Religion."

About ten minutes into Brother Maddox's sermon, I started nodding. A roar of "Amens" from the Brothers' side jolted me awake. When Preacher Maddox really got wound up, the "Amens" rolled over the Brothers' side like distant thunder.

Brother Maddox was warning of the judgment and the hereafter one morning when he shouted, "And youah all goin' ta Hell _." I'm sure he was going to add, "if yuh don't repent an' believe the gospel." But old Mr. Simmons, snapped awake and hollered, "AMEN!" before the preacher finished his sentence. The ensuing laughter ruined the effect of the sermon and Brother Maddox moved into the "invitation" very quickly.

Times were hard and the offerings slim in those days. Brother Maddox and his family lived on thin rations. Come Sunday, and they feasted. After checking with Grandmother, Daddy Floyd would edge up to Brother Maddox. "Preachah, if yuh don't mind eatin' with po' folks, bring youah missus and chirren and come and take dinnah with us."

Sunday Dinner at the Floyds, in the midst of the Great Depression, meant fried chicken, mashed potatoes with milk gravy, sliced tomatoes, turnips and greens, black-eyed peas, boiled okra, corn bread and buttermilk. They're all still favorites of mine except boiled okra. Daddy Floyd never could get me to eat that slimy stuff.

Sunday evening, we got leftovers, then we all piled in the wagon and Daddy Floyd drove us back to church. The next morning we began a new work week.

Winter, spring, summer and fall, every day of the week, Daddy Floyd could always be counted on to bring joy and togetherness to our family. On the coldest winter nights, he provided our after-dinner entertainment.

We generally gathered around the fireplace in his and Grandmother's big bedroom to parch peanuts and pop popcorn, and listen to Daddy Floyd's stories and songs. My favorite was "Ole Dan Tucker" and Daddy Floyd knew a zillion verses to it. Like,

Ole Dan Tucker was a goin' to town,
Riding a goat and leadin' a hound,
The hound gave a bark, the goat gave a jump,
And threw Dan Tucker right straddle a stump.

On summer evenings we moved out to the porch to sit in rockers and straight-back chairs. I don't think there was a star in the sky whose name Daddy Floyd didn't know.

"Look up theah, Jimmie. See those seven stahs that look like a dippah? Those stahs are called the Big Dippah. Now follah in a line from those two stahs in the dippah handle — see the No'th Stah?"

He moved on to other stars, naming them and all their constellations. Sometimes he dotted stars on a piece of paper and drew lines so we could see why the ancients had named them the way they had. He also planted his crops by the positions of the stars in the sky and by the moon phases.

He made all sorts of toys and puzzles for us. My favorite was a "hummer," consisting of a six-foot long stick to which he attached a three-foot string. To the end of the string, he tied a flat piece of wood about an inch wide, a quarter inch thick and a foot long. When you swung the long stick around your head, the flat piece of wood emitted a low hum. Doris and I ran all around the front yard, swinging our hummers, trying to hit lightening bugs while Daddy Floyd, Grandmother and Helen Maude cheered us on.

Daddy Floyd was special. He was the "star" that kept my young life "humming."

Chapter 8

"Grandmother"

Doris and I were talking birthdays with Grandmother when she looked up from putting a pan of dough in the oven. "Ah was born on a girl's day — Ada May. Do you chirrun know what day that is?"

Doris grinned knowingly. I shook my head in puzzlement.

"Eighth of May, eighteen-and-eighty two, over at the Armstrong place, jus' a couple of miles from here," Grandmother said. Ah was born during the year of the big flood on the Mississippi. John M. Stone was Governor of Mississippi an' Chester A. Arthur was President of the United States."

"Adah May," I murmured, finally catching on, but not caring about the ancient history.

Grandmother recited the years of our births: "Daddy Floyd in 1881, Ruth in 1904, Cecil in 1906, Vernell in 1911, Lamar — God rest his soul, in 1915." She blinked, then continued. "Helen Maude in 1918, Doris in 1923, and you, Jimmie, in 1924."

Grandmother didn't like to talk about the child she had lost. But we were reminded every Sunday morning when she walked across the road from the church and stood over his grave, meditating and remembering the saddest day of her life, the day Lamar left her and "went to be with Jesus."

"Her grief was so profound," a neighbor lady, Mrs. Joyce Moore, told me later, "that one night she slipped out of her bed an' began aimlessly walking. Early in the morning she was found eight miles from home an' taken to the nearest farm. Luckily it belonged to your Uncle Lonnie.

"Youah Uncle Lonnie, Jimmie, knew youah grandfathah would be almost out of his mind with worry about her, so he sent one of his boys racin' tow'd youah house on his fastest horse. Youah Uncle Lonnie followed with youah grandmothah in the buggy an' they met youah grandfathah about four miles from hoam. Youah Grandfathah Floyd wept like a child when they were reunited."

Mrs. Moore said she shared with Grandmother the loss of her first two children to typhoid fever. After much consoling Grandmother finally tore the grief out of her heart through wrenching sobs. I'm sure the pain never lessened one iota but she was able to bear it. I had no way to gauge the depths of her suffering until my first-born son passed away suddenly years later. Then I knew. I knew.

Miz Jennie, as everybody outside our family called Grandmother, taught school a couple of years before marriage and would have continued if the school board had rehired her. The board took the position that married women would shortly be mothers and should not work outside the home.

Not that Grandmother stopped teaching. While she spoke the brogue of east-central Mississippi, she kept her ear cocked for incorrect speech.

Vernell's young wife, Angie, hadn't been brought up to speak properly. One sweltering June afternoon she commented to Grandmother, "Hit looks lack hit's goin' ta rain. Don't yuh think so, Mothah?"

"IT, not hit, Angie. IT looks as if IT is going to rain."

Angie teared up a little. "Ah know that, Mothah, but Ah keep forgettin'."

"Ah'll hep yuh remember," Grandmother promised.

That night Grandmother tacked a sign above every door in the house bearing just one word, IT.

"Jus' b'cause we'ah not rich an' didn't go to college dudden mean we have to talk like trash," she explained.

Not that Grandmother wasn't expressive. Her older brother, Bob, was a timber estimator, who walked through stands of timber and estimated the board feet of the finished lumber. Uncle Bob could come so close in his estimates it was uncanny. He was a remarkable man in his profession, but to Grandmother he was just plain "Bob, the tree totaller."

Grandmother was a farm lady who worked the year 'round. During planting and harvesting times, she toiled in the fields with Daddy Floyd from sunup to sundown, leaving me in Aunt Lizzie's tender care.

Every farm family had a vegetable garden. Daddy Floyd and Grandmother's covered almost ten acres. "We named it Devil's Half Acre," Daddy Floyd said, "because the land was so 'devilish' to clear of trees. Dynamite, at a dime a stick, was too blamed expensive back then. We had to dig 'round the stumps and pull them out with the brute power of men, mules and oxen. Then we had to break up the roots with big middlebuster plows."

Daddy Floyd and his hired men did the regular farm work. He and Grandmother planted the garden with 'Ish potatoes, sweet potatoes, turnips, onions, squash and other vegetables that kept well without refrigeration. Grandmother then hoed and tended the plants until harvest.

Needy people who lived in Hickory and other nearby towns looked forward to harvest time at Devil's Half Acre. Black or white, any needy person who didn't have a farm could take away all the vegetables they could carry from the garden. They could come back in a week, but again, they could make just one trip out of the garden. That was my grandparents' inflexible rule for their home-made welfare program.

People came pushing wheelbarrows and pulling goat carts. One family walked all the way from Meridian, pulling a tattered old buggy. They slept at night along the road.

When a family would load up, the father would sidle up to Daddy Floyd and Grandmother and say,

"Mistah James and Miz Jennie, we'ah mighty grateful to yuh for sharin' your abundance with us. Now we'd like to do a little work to pay yuh back."

My grandparents could always find a couple of hours work to pay for the vegetables — "to allow them to keep their dignity," Grandmother said.

After a long day in the fields, Grandmother came home and helped Daddy Floyd milk eight cows before supper. The cats followed her into the milk lot behind the barn and waited expectantly as she brushed back her long skirt to take a position on the stool.

The cats serenaded with a chorus of meows. When Grandmother squirted a stream straight into an old tom's open mouth, I would clap my hands in glee. "Right on the money, Grandmothah."

Squirt, squirt, squirt into the pail. Squirt for a cat's mouth ten feet away. I laughed. Grandmother grinned. The cats chorused their meows. The cows flicked their tails at the swarm of pesky horse flies buzzing over their backs.

I ventured close and began grabbing flies. When I got a handful I stepped back and stripped off their wings. Then I ran into the barn and flipped the helpless creatures to the big toads that lived under the harness room. The toads flicked their tongues and the horse flies simply disappeared. The toads were the best fed creatures on the farm.

By Grandmother's rule, every creature had its place and a dog definitely did not belong in the house, or even on the back porch. Not that she didn't appreciate our canine guards. She just didn't want them around our living quarters.

Daddy Floyd always bought his dogs from a man in Meridian who bred an English bulldog with shepherds. They were ideal farm dogs with a strong protective instinct that flared when canines from neighboring farms ventured into their assigned territory.

Daddy Floyd liked dogs, but showed no imagination at all with names. He alternated between "Sport" and "Doc." The mixed breed he assigned to me happened to be a "Sport." Daddy Floyd taught my Sport to bring the cows up from the swamp pasture, to guard all the farm animals, and most important to me, to hate snakes.

Once Sport and I were coming along the road from Hickory toward the house when a deadly poisonous, cotton mouth moccasin crossed ahead of us. Sport saw the reptile and was off like a shot.

He reached the snake just as it left the roadside ditch and entered the woods. I ran to help him with the hoe I carried. As I approached warily I saw Sport coming, clutching the snake in his jaws and shaking it violently.

Sport saw me and abruptly stopped shaking the cotton mouth in such a way that the snake's head was stretched out toward me!

Whack! One quick chop and off came the cottonmouth's head. I hoped Sport had escaped the snake's fangs but we hadn't gone fifty yards when I saw my dog's head begin to swell. He escorted me home, all the way into the backyard, then turned and slunk off into the cornfield.

"Heah, Sport, heah, boy," I called from the back porch.

Grandmother came to the back door. "Hush, Jimmie. 'fo yuh know it, that dog will be wantin' to come in the house."

"But Grandmother," I pleaded. "He kept me from gettin' bit by a cottonmouth."

Grandmother came out and looked me over good. "You appear to be all right to me."

"Yes, Grandmother, but the snake bit Sport. He might even die."

"Well, yuh can't hep him now, Jimmie. Come on in the house. Yuh look tired."

The next morning, I ran out in the yard, calling Sport. Ordinarily he would have come bounding up. I raced to the barn. I looked and called everywhere I could think he might be. No Sport.

He didn't show up the second day, nor the third. On the morning of the fourth, I had about given up hope when I heard a yip, yip, yip. I turned and saw him bounding across the cornfield, tail wagging, head up. He ran into the yard and started toward the back porch where I was standing. I was so glad to see him I didn't think to shoo him away. Grandmother came charging out of the kitchen, waving her broom over her head. Poor Sport was no dummy and scooted away as fast as his legs could carry him.

I ran after him into the cornfield. "Sport! Sport!." Not until he got out of Grandmother's sight did he whirl and come back to me. I hugged him and kissed him. My dog was alive!

He followed me back into the yard. When he got close to the house, I hollered, "Get away, Sport, 'fo Grandmothah sees yuh." He obediently began backing up.

Grandmother didn't hate dogs. She just didn't want them in "her" territory.

Grandmother's values were as flawless as Daddy Floyd's. Once when I was about eight I walked with her a mile and a half to visit Mrs. Harris, a well-to-do lady who lived in a fine house on the other side of Okhatta Creek. Mrs. Harris's children happened not to be there and I played with their toys.

A small cast iron tractor captured my heart. I played with it all afternoon. I knew I could never have one like it since it cost twenty-five cents. I wanted that tractor more than anything in the whole wide world and when we left I took it with me.

I kept it out of Grandmother's sight, or so I believed. When we got home, I excused myself to go play on the cool ground under the house. I was "zoom-zooming" the tractor back and forth when I looked around and saw Grandmother down on her knees watching me.

"Jimmie, wheah did yuh get that toy?" she asked in a soft voice.

I was suddenly stricken with guilt. My eyelids dropped. "Ah got it at the Harris' house. Ah didn't think them rich boys would miss it."

She said those fearful words: "Well, come on out an' let's take it back." We had already walked three miles that day, but she knew clearly what we had to do.

We didn't speak all the way to the Harris house, and as we reached the yard I tried a quick sell. "Ah'll jus run on up an' put it back while yuh wait heah."

It was worth trying, but it didn't work. "No, Jimmie, you'll have to go up youahsef an' apologize."

I thought I'd die from embarrassment but I stammered tearfully through an apology. We walked back home in miserable silence, with Grandmother staying five feet away from me the whole way. As we climbed the red clay slope to our house she moved close and reached out an arm. As our hands touched I began to cry. She stopped, knelt down before me, and I threw my arms around her neck.

"Oh, Grandmothah," I sobbed, "Ah thought yuh wudden love me any moah."

She folded her arms about me and held me close. "Ah'll always love yuh, Jimmie, but maybe sometimes Ah won't love what yuh do."

She never mentioned the incident to Daddy Floyd and I was glad because I didn't want to break his heart. She loved me so much that she walked those three extra miles to show me how important it is to confess a wrong. I gave up my career as a master thief. It hadn't been any fun.

Grandmother believed in manners, too.

One time the new lawyer in Hickory took his son to the head of the food line at a political gathering and lifted him over the lane ropes. Grandmother watched frowning.

Without saying a word, she pushed her way up the line, picked up the boy and carried him gently back to his father at the end of the line. Turning to the frowning lawyer, she said, "Max Ladt, yuh don't have any mannahs or cultuah atall."

Most people must have agreed with her because Max didn't linger long in Hickory.

For me, as a young boy, Grandmother seemed invincible. (I didn't learn about her reaction to Lamar's death until years later.) Invincible, until one day I playfully shut the door of one of our big walk-in closets on her.

"Jimmie," she wailed, "open this doah an' let me out. Now!"

I pretended not to hear her.

"Jimmie, please open the doah. Please." She was pleading almost like a child.

I opened the door and she rushed out. "Don't yuh evah do that to me again. I can't stand to have a door closed on me in a dark place."

Years later I learned that she had claustrophobia. She also felt insecure in an automobile.

She started off right. Daddy Floyd taught her to drive a Model T a year or so after I was born. This creation of Henry Ford's didn't have a shift transmission but used a planetary gear arrangement that was really a forerunner of the much later automatic transmission.

There were three pedals on the floor in addition to the accelerator pedal. To go forward the driver pushed the left pedal to the floor and released it slowly while pressing the accelerator pedal. To go in reverse the driver pushed down on the middle pedal and released it while pressing the accelerator pedal. The third pedal was the brake.

Shortly after learning to drive, Grandmother motored to the storefront bank in Hickory to do some business for Daddy Floyd. "You chirrun stay in the car," she instructed Doris and me. "Ah'll only be a minute."

We could see her watching us through the big plate glass window as she chatted with Florene Haley, one of the tellers. Grandmother later told the family what Miss Haley said when she turned to leave: "Yuh come back real soon, now yuh heah, Miz Jennie."

Grandmother slid behind the wheel of the Model T. She had parked at a 45 degree angle to the curb, as is common practice in many small towns, and was going to back out into the street.

Unfortunately, she pressed the wrong pedal. The car began moving forward instead of backward.

She panicked and "floored" the accelerator pedal. In an instant the car, with Grandmother, Doris and me inside, soared like a big mechanical bird through the plate glass bank window. Amidst the sounds of screeching tires and broken glass, we heard screams and shouts.

The silence that followed was broken by the small voice of Miss Haley: "Ah didden mean that soon, Miz Jennie."

That ended Grandmother's love affair with automobiles. From that day forward she had an unreasoning fear of cars and speed.

She simply refused to ride with speeders. No matter where we were driving, whether on dirt roads or concrete, Grandmother knew when Daddy Floyd was driving over thirty miles an hour. She gave him two miles an hour grace, then she spoke fearfully, "Floyd!"

It was uncanny. Even if she was looking out the window she knew exactly how fast the car was going. Daddy Floyd didn't get upset with her. He just reached over and patted her knee and said, "All right, Jennie," and slowed down to thirty miles an hour.

My grandparents' farm was located in the tornado belt. Grandmother was afraid of closed places, high places and of speeding cars, but when it looked like we might get a bad storm the most she might say was, "Well, Ah speck we bettah get the clothes off the gahden fence, an' Jimmie, yuh bettah put Sport in the preserves room. Now make haste an' get back in the house; it's gonna get windy an' rainy right quick."

We could tell by how the air felt when a blow was coming. The chickens stopped clucking and retreated to their roost. The wild birds vanished. The wind ceased and the air hung heavily over the house. I felt the hair raise on my neck.

Most storms moved on us from the west and we watched them coming from our front porch which faced in that direction. It was eerie to stand in perfect stillness and see a wide, dark cloud, dispensing rain in sheets, advancing across the fields. Many times we didn't feel any wind until the rain was barely 200 yards away.

One April afternoon — I think it was in 1935 — my aunts and I were playing near the barn, when I heard Grandmother holler, "Stohm! Stohm! Get back to the house, chirrun."

Helen Maude, Doris and I joined Grandmother and Daddy Floyd on the front porch and watched the black cloud approach. When the wind-driven rain began peppering our faces, we slipped inside.

Other people I knew sought refuge in their storm cellar. I asked Daddy Floyd once why we didn't have one and he said, "Why, yuh know if yuh jus' think about it, Jimmie."

When I still looked puzzled he simply said, "Storm cellars ah real tight places an' youah grandmothah would soonah be blown away than hide in a hole."

Even so, Grandmother took storms seriously. She could never forget April 5, 1936, when a series of tornadoes swept across parts of Mississippi and Georgia. Thankfully, we escaped the worst part of that terrible storm.

Not until after the storm front had swept past did we learn that 455 people were killed. This still stands as the second worst tornado disaster in American history.

Grandmother may have had her foibles, but she also had her principles and loyalties.

Next to God, her first loyalty was to her family. When I cried for Mother she comforted me. When we knew Mother was coming, Grandmother helped me count the days.

In Care of the Conductor

When Mother stepped off the train in Meridian, Grandmother, along with Daddy Floyd, made sure I was there. When Daddy Floyd took Mother back to the Meridian station, Grandmother went along. When Mother assured me that she was going to marry the man of her dreams, so I could again live with her, Grandmother nodded her approval.

Whatever happened, I knew I could count on Grandmother.

Chapter 9

"Doctor Gilmore"

I had two physicians: Grandmother and Doc Gilmore.

March brought warm winds and Grandmother's annual announcement: "It's that time of yeah again, chirren."

I knew what Grandmother had in mind: Black Draught, the foulest brew ever concocted by man or beast. Grandmother administered it just before bedtime, leaving me to grab frantically for the sweet lemonade that awaited as a reward.

This devil's brew was supposed to froth, ferment and boil the insides of my stomach during the night, preparing me for an early morning stroll to the two-holer near the hog pasture fence.

Black Draught never worked that way for me. Most times I scarcely made it halfway, as I ran "stretched out an' belly to the groun'."

Once when I fell short, Daddy Floyd commented, "Yuh know, Jimmie, Ah heard that a boy down in Jasper County made it all the way to the outhouse with time to spaah this yeah. They must be makin' Black Draught weaker now."

They really weren't making the stuff weaker that year. I should have known I wouldn't make it to the outhouse when I saw the wash tub filled with water.

"Sulphah an'…" was Grandmother's year-round weapon of choice. It might be sulphur and yellow soap, sulphur and coal oil, sulphur and Vaseline, or any of a dozen other combinations, all beginning, "Sulpha an'…"

Thanks to "sulphah'…an'," skeeters shied away from me in the swamps, while they ate alive the hunters from Meridian who ventured there. Twenty years later a chemist in St. Louis told me that the sulphur in my body was expelled through my pores as sulphur dioxide. I literally stunk so much that I ruined the skeeters' appetite.

When Grandmother got desperate she sent for Doc Gilmore, the Hickory physician who presided at my birth. During the great malaria epidemic of 1934, Doc practically lived in his car, even stopping on the road to take short naps as he drove from house to house. When he came to our place, he excused himself to run to his car for "some moah medicine" — translation, "a long swig of Scotch." Grandmother, who hated strong drink with a passion, went along with his pretense.

The fever pervaded my ten-year-old body. The memory of the piercing headaches is vivid to this hour. I cried for Mother, but her boss wouldn't give her time off to come and visit her critically ill son.

Grandmother kept vigil, calling on Doc Gilmore during the darkest moments. Grandmother stayed by my cot day and night, constantly bathing me down with cool well water to keep the fever from soaring out of control. My rival, Doris, didn't realize the seriousness of my illness. "The reason Jimmie acts so strange," she told Helen Maude, "is 'cause the malaria cooked his brain — what there is left of it." Sweet Helen Maude didn't think that funny at all.

The malaria epidemic finally subsided and the rains came, sending the overflow from Chunky River into the swamp. I felt good enough to join other boys on nature's own roller coaster. We found we could jump off the Chunky River bridge at 16th Road and ride high, wide and handsome on the raging flood through the swamp to the new Highway 80 bridge six miles away. It was exciting fun; we just had to be careful not to get sucked into the whirlpools under fallen trees.

I didn't consider the consequences of the muddy water leaking into my ears. The morning after one especially wild ride, my ears began pulsating with pain.

"Grandmothah! Oh, Grandmothah!" I screeched.

She pulled me to the window for an inspection. "Jimmie, have you been wallowin' with the hogs? No wonduh youah eahs hurt so bad. Thea'ah all caked with mud. Thea'ah probably infected too.

She touched one ear gently.

"Owwww, owwww," I moaned.

She tried her hot oil treatment for a couple of days. When the pain kept me from sleeping at night, she called Daddy Floyd. "Crank up the Foad. We'ah takin' Jimmie to Doc Gilmore."

The Ford bounced and splashed along the muddy road to Hickory. Grandmother held on to me for dear life as I groaned in her arms. "Dear Lawd, let Doc be in his office," she prayed. "Dear Lawd, let him be sober foah jus' once."

Daddy Floyd turned the corner on to Jefferson Street and gently coasted to a stop in front of Doc Gilmore's little office building. He jumped out to receive me from Grandmother's arms and they raced inside.

Daddy Floyd stood me down. "Doc? Doctah Gilmore?" he called.

The doctor came staggering out of a back room, his eyes bleary, his speech turned to mush. He bowed slightly to Grandmother and nodded at Daddy Floyd.

"It's our grandson's ears, Doc," Grandmother said. "Thea'ah infected from mud."

His eyes lit on me. "Miz Jennie, yuh an' Floyd jus' stay heah while Ah have a look at Jimmie's ears."

Doc led me into his examining room and set me on a chair. "Youah eahs hurt bad, boy?"

I moaned loudly for extra effect and bobbed my head. Never had I felt such terrible, throbbing pain.

He peered inside both ears. He poked gently, then withdrew and walked back to see Daddy Floyd and Grandmother. "Yoah granboy, heah, has got bad abscesses in both ears. Ah'll have to lance the drums. It's too close to the brain to give him anesthesia."

Daddy Floyd and Grandmother gave their consent.

The doctor returned to me, rolling his bleary eyes. "Jus' hold real still, son. This is gonna hurt a little, but Ah'll get it ovah with real quick."

He slipped a slender scalpel into my right ear and made a tiny flick. I felt a slight pop, accompanied by a warm gushing. The pain was nothing compared to what I had felt on the way into town. Now I felt no pain at all in this ear.

My left ear still throbbed. I had been fearful of what he'd do with the other ear. Now I hurried the doctor for fear he'd pass out before finishing the treatment. He staggered around to my other side and repeated the action.

"Feel bettah?"

"Uh, huh," I mumbled.

"Ah'm not through yet, son. Ah'm gonna wash all that ole crud out of yoah ears."

He syringed my ears out with peroxide, then took two wobbly steps back and opened a cabinet door to drink from a bottle. "Ah need a little treatment, mahself."

He put the bottle back and escorted me back to my grandparents. Grandmother frowned as she saw him come weaving into the waiting room.

"Jimmie's all fixed up," he said. "Yuh can take him back home now. If his ears staht hurtin' ag'in, bring 'im back to mah office."

Daddy Floyd handed the doctor his payment. Grandmother forced a smile as she said, "Thank yuh, Doctah." She didn't deride him for his drunkenness.

With his alcoholism, I don't know how Doc Gilmore lived as long as he did. Even when drunk, he was a magnificent surgeon. Five or six years after he saved my ears, I was loafing in the Hickory square with some buddies my age when I heard a plaintive voice. An old black man had stopped his wagon and was pleading for help for a neighbor he had brought into town.

I called my friends and we walked ahead of the wagon to Doc Gilmore's office. Pitiful groans were clearly audible from the man lying in the bed of the wagon. "Young Mistuh," the driver implored me, "could yuh and yoah friends carry po' George in to see the doctah. George got kicked by a mule."

Another boy and I jumped in the wagon. An awful stench assailed us. The old man's discolored right bare foot looked as if it was about to rot off. Somehow we managed to lift him up and over the wagon bed to our two buddies who stood on the ground. The four of us lugged George into Doc Gilmore's office. The wagon driver said he would wait outside.

Doc Gilmore stumbled in from a back room, rubbing his blood-shot eyes, and saw the old black man lying on the floor. "Shoosh, whatta we got heah, boys?

I explained how we had happened to bring George to Doc's office, and that he had been kicked by a mule.

Doc bent over to check his pulse, then raised up, shaking his head.

The old man opened his eyes and grinned. "Mah laig hurts awful bad, Doctah. That mule sho kin kick."

"Ah'm gonna take care of you, uncle," Doc promised. "Carry him into mah surgery room an' put him on the table, boys."

Doc Gilmore cut off George's tattered denim overalls on his right leg below the hip. The leg looked worse than the patient's foot.

"Gangrene," Doc solemnly pronounced. "Ah'll hafta to remove youah leg, uncle."

"Whatevah yuh say, Doctah."

Doc dropped a cloth over his patient's face and started the ether drip. "Yuh boys may not want to stay aroun' foah this. Ah'll take good care of youah friend."

We didn't have to be told a second time. "We'll wait outside," I said.

Late that afternoon Doc came stumbling out. He had obviously had more to drink. "How's ole George?" I asked.

Doc rolled his eyes. "Ah took off his right leg. Ah'm gonna have ta watch him awhile longah. Yuh boys might as well go on hoam."

The wagon driver came over from where he had been resting in the shade of a magnolia tree. We gave him Doc's report.

"Ah was afeart he mout lose his leg. Ah've gotta be gittin' back. Ah'll come back tomorrah an' bring George home."

We drifted away to other interests. The next day I dropped by Doc's office. "Ah've still got 'im back theah," he said. Doc lurched over to his wall cabinet for another drink.

Doc kept George for two more days before turning him loose.

The patient survived.

Doc Gilmore lived on for a few more years, a slave to alcohol to his dying day. Among other things, he left three shoe boxes full of uncollected bills which he forgave in his will.

I don't remember that he had a single living relative, but many people, including my grandparents, mourned his passing.

There's a street named Gilmore in Hickory today.

"Poah Doc Gilmore," Grandmother often lamented. "He hept so many folks, but he couldn't hep himself."

Chapter 10

"Swamp Boys"

It was one of those hot, humid, sweltering times in late summer that Grandmother called "the dog days." I snoozed in the front porch swing, in cut-off "ovahhauls", my head pinched against the arm rest and one foot on the opposite chain. The swing moved rhythmically from side to side, propelled by the intermittent pressing of my foot on the chain.

In my dream Mother had married a loving, handsome man and we were living together on the farm. In my hazy imagination I did not separate him from my birth father whom Mother had said would not be coming back.

Mother was bragging about my school work. "Ah'm so proud of yuh, Jimmie, Ah could jus' bust."

My fantasy was interrupted by a gentle, boyish voice. "Hey, Jimmie?"

I opened one eye and there standing on the ground and leaning against the porch was George Snowden.

George was three years older, but in the third grade with me. He didn't take to "book learnin' " very well and I often helped him with his homework.

He was the only son of the white sharecrop family who lived on our place. He was already doing a man's work on the farm and I guess he came by it naturally because I never saw his daddy idle, except on Sunday.

"Hey, George. How come you'ah not in the field," I said.

"It's Saturday an' Pa tole me Ah could lay out whilst him an' youah gran'daddy went to Hickory."

George's voice was uncommonly soft and he spoke with a measured slow drawl. His eyes were light blue and set in a square face above a straight nose and a large friendly mouth. He wore a straw hat crammed down to flatten the tops of his ears. Under the hat I knew there was a shock of uncombed white hair. All the time I knew him, I never saw it combed. George wore a perpetual smile with teeth too large for his mouth. It gave him a sort of a monkey look. We were very best friends.

I never saw him angry and there were times he should have been. Like when JT Gibbs tried to fight him at school. JT didn't stand for the initials of his name, JT was his name. JT's daddy knew a judge with those initials and it sounded so good to him that he named his son JT.

Mistaking George's gentleness for cowardice, JT decided to bully and humiliate my buddy in front of the other boys. George took JT's insults for about two weeks and then he turned to JT one day at dinner time and said in that soft drawl of his, "Awright, JT, Ah reckon Ah'll hafta satisfy yuh."

I looked at George's face expecting to see it distorted in anger, but it wasn't. JT came at him, swinging like a windmill. JT had the reputation of being the best fighter in grade school and I was afraid for George. But I needn't have been. All George did was wrap his arms around JT and bear hug him. JT began beating on George's back with his fists but George kept his head pressed down to JT's chest and held him up so his feet didn't touch the ground.

After about a minute JT could barely hold his head up. His face turned from purple to a frightening white. The rest of us had been hollering and screaming and enjoying the fight but now we were all frightened into silence. The realization hit us that we were witnessing a boy being slowly killed.

One of the older boys tried to stop George but it was like he was a bull dog and had JT in a death grip. Finally, the older boy ran over to me, fright written all over his face.

"Jimmie, you'ah the only one George will listen to. Make him stop before he kills JT." By now I was half scared out of my skin. But I ran over and grabbed George and started shaking him wildly.

"Please, George, stop it right now! JT's had 'nuf!"

George seemed not to hear me. He still had his head on JT's chest and was squeezing for all he was worth. JT's arms and head were hanging limp and his eyes were rolled back in his head.

"Stop it, George! You'ah killing JT!"

George must have heard me this time. He dropped JT to the ground and grabbed me!

"No, George!" I screamed. Then I realized I was crying wildly and that George was only trying to help me. "Ah'm all right, George. It's JT that's hurt."

JT was lying on his back, gasping for air. George looked down at him for a moment, then stepped a'straddle of JT with one foot on each side. Bending at the waist, George caught JT with both hands and began a form of artificial resuscitation I've never seen since. Over and over, George pulled him up and then let him fall back level again until JT began to breathe naturally. By the end of dinner time JT was able to walk to afternoon classes, but he had to lean on George.

George's voice on this lazy day of summer broke in on my thoughts and brought me up to the present.

"D'yuh wanna go fishin', Jimmie?"

"Ah reckon so. Wheah'll we go?"

"That ole slough down b'low the east paschah's got fish in it."

I touched my bare feet to the floor, stood up and stretched.

George grabbed a couple of tin cans and a hoe from Daddy Floyd's shop. "C'mon, Jimmie, the fish ah waitin' foah us."

"Wait till I get Sport." I called but my dog didn't respond.

"Let's go, Jimmie. Sport's prob'ly out chasin' a rabbit."

I followed George down into the pasture where it sloped toward the slough at the edge of the swamp. We found a spot where the ground was moist and we could see small mounds of grey earth balls indicating the presence of redworms below ground. We dug at least a hundred, then moved over to the slough.

At mid-day it was shady-dark in the deep woods. Shafts of light stabbed through the overhead trees to the leafy floor, making the shade seem even darker. The swamp was a quiet, peaceful place.

George cut us two tall, thin hickory saplings for fishing poles. He trimmed the branches from the poles with his hand-me-down pocket knife, then pulled from his pocket two balls of string, and tied the end of each string to a sapling. He had already tied hooks to the other ends of the strings and wrapped sheet lead about six inches above the hooks.

He pulled two molasses jug corks from his pocket, tied them about three feet above the hooks and handed one of the poles to me. Reaching into one of the cans, he selected a juicy, fat worm and threaded it on my hook. After it was wiggling on the hook he eyed it critically and then spit on it.

"What's that foah?" I asked.

"Ah dunno," he responded, "but Pa says it draws fish."

I'd been fishing before with Doris, but I'd never caught much, mainly because she didn't know beans about the sport and could care less. I couldn't have been taught by anyone more skilled than George at this time in my life.

I wanted to swing the baited hook out in the middle of the slough but George told me to fish alongside an old sunken log tapering from the bank out into the slough. "Fish hide wheah they kin find bugs and worms."

I swung my line a few feet out and let the bait drop beside the old log. The bait hadn't even touched bottom when my pole dipped. Instinctively, I pulled back and felt the fish.

"Ah've got one!" I yelled.

George's big mouth spread wide. "Wael bring it in."

In my excitement, I jerked too hard and slung the little catfish over my head and into the limb of a willow tree behind me.

I turned and looked up at my trophy dangling from the willow. "Ah cain't reach it, George."

Without a word, George leaped and grabbed the limb, pulling it down to where I could get the fish. It wasn't much longer than my hand, but the way my heart was pounding, you'd have thought I'd caught one as long as Daddy Floyd's leg.

I stood there holding the slimy little catfish in my right hand, wondering what I should do next.

"Don't let it stick you," George warned. "I'll cut a stringer." He clipped off a hickory branch that had the natural shape of a Y, leaving one of the upper arms about three feet long. "A Choctaw Indian showed me how to do this," George explained. "Gimme youah fish."

He threaded the long branch through the catfish's gills and out his mouth. Then he jabbed the end about six inches into the mud at the edge of the slough, leaving the fish gurgling in the water.

I baited my hook this time. By the time I had my line back in the water, George was pulling out a cat twice the size of the one I'd caught.

My pole dipped again. This time I caught a perch.

George strung it behind his fish. The next fish almost jerked me into the dark water. I hollered, loud enough to be heard half way to Hickory, "Ah cain't hold this 'un, George."

The fish was runnin' first one way and then the other. I was barely hanging on when George grabbed the pole above my wrist. "Ah figures that's an ole bass," he said. "Let it weah itself out, oah it'll break youah line."

George extended the pole out as far over the water as he could, then pulled back gently. The bass reversed itself and ran towards us. Then it tried to duck under the log. George pulled it away and handed the pole back to me. "Keep the line tight, Jimmie. It'll get tiahd in a minute."

George was right. After two or three more sweeps the bass fell limp and I dragged it in. George slipped his finger in a gill and lifted up my trophy. "A two-pounder, foah sho."

We kept catching fish, right and left. Our bait would no sooner start sinking toward the bottom when something would grab it. Within an hour we filled up one stringer, then a second.

"We'd bettah get these fish home," George grunted.

"Aw, cain't we stay a little longah?"

George shook his head. "If we take moah than we can eat, we'll be wastin' fish. We've gotta save some foah the nex' time."

We gathered up the stringers and strutted back to the house. Daddy Floyd had not returned from

Hickory, but Grandmother was there and saw us coming.

She came trotting out to welcome us. George held up the big bass. "Jimmie caught this'un and a lot moah," he said proudly.

Grandmother looked our strings up and down. "Yuh boys did youahseves proud."

I puffed out my bare chest. "We only fished an ouah oah two."

George took one string home with him. "Where do Ah put mah string?" I asked Grandmother.

"You take them out back an' clean them," she said.

My face fell. "Ah'll never get 'um all cleaned."

Grandmother flashed a warm smile. "Jus' think how proud youah grandaddy will be when he sees all those fish ready foah the pan. C'mon, Ah'll hep yuh get stahted."

Grandmother showed me how to clean the first fish and I cleaned the rest. It took me over an hour, but I finished. It helped when Daddy Floyd prayed over the food and thanked God not only for having a grandson who knew how to catch fish but also for cleaning them so willingly.

Besides showing me how to catch more fish, George took me deeper into the Okahatta swamp woods than I had ever been before, even as far as Chestnut Island. On the way there, we threaded our way through a rich forest of trees: scalybark hickory, three kinds of oak, willow, walnut, cypress, cottonwood, tupelo, sweet gum, sassafras, and my favorite, the majestic, towering magnolia with its cloyingly sweet blossoms. The low growing trees and bushes included huckleberry, hazelnut, redbud, dogwood, holly and laurel. George knew the names of most of these and if we found one he didn't know we'd take a branch home for Daddy Floyd to identify. He never failed us.

When George couldn't go fishing and exploring, I went by myself. Once I brought home a branch with some curious spiny knots containing nuts on the limbs. Grandmother, surprised, said, "Wheah'd yuh get that, Jimmie?"

"Down in the swamp. Why?"

"Nevah mind jus' now."

But that night at the supper table she said to my grandfather with concern, "Floyd, did yuh know Jimmie has been all the way to Chestnut Island by himself?"

Chestnut Island stood about ten feet higher than the rest of the swamp and was so named because it was the only place where chestnut trees grew. "Island" only applied when the Okahatta flooded the swamp, leaving the elevation high and dry. Barely five acres in size, it was located over a mile and a half from our house in the most dense part of the swamp.

Daddy Floyd looked at me intently. "Does it look lack theah'll be many nuts this fall?"

Before I could answer Grandmother said somewhat peevishly, "But Floyd, don't yuh think tha's too fah in the swamp foah him to go? He might get lost."

Daddy Floyd turned to me with sort of a twitch around his mouth.

"Boy, did yuh get lost?"

"No suh, but theah were times Ah didn't rightly know where Ah was. Ah jus' listened foah Uncle Ban's bull or foah a cow bell. If Ah couldn't heah them, Ah looked wheah the sun was an' Ah knew which way was hoam."

Daddy Floyd looked at me for a long moment and then at Grandmother, saying gently, "Jennie, don't you think the most important thing foah him to know is the way hoam? If we teach him right, he'll always know the way hoam."

After that Grandmother never seemed to worry about me, except to see that I took a little sack of food and a fruit jar full of water when I went down to the swamp woods. And she saw that I took Sport along when he wasn't off on one of his rabbit expeditions.

George went with me when he could. He and I discovered pools swarming with fish in the swampy woods that I'm sure had never been fished before. We fished any way we could to get fish. On days they wouldn't bite we took the hoes we carried to kill cotton mouth moccasins and tried to jerk the fish out of the pools. We also tried to rake fish out of shallow pools, with disappointing results. We splashed out a few small ones but we got so muddy that Grandmother pretended she didn't know me when we got to the house.

Daddy Floyd told us to always be on the lookout for a line of bees. "When they get theah fill of nectah," he said, "they head foah thuh hive. When yuh find one, make a lick trail that we can follah to find the bee tree."

One warm August afternoon George and I saw a bee flying in a straight line. We ran to the spot where we saw it last and waited. Sure enough another bee came flying past and we chased it till it was out of sight. Then we heard the hummmmm.

"Theah 'tis, Jimmie." George pointed up.

I was already under the big white oak. Bees were swarming in a cloud above me and I could see them going inside a hole in the trunk about thirty feet up. "They've got a big hive up theah," I told George, "an' Ah bet it's full of sweet honey."

George had brought along his half ax, thinking we might find a hive. On the way home, he took a lick out of trees every hundred feet or so along the way to mark a trail.

We ran into the shop where Daddy Floyd was bent over his forge. "We found a hive!" I hollered.

He looked around in interest. "Did yuh make a lick trail?"

"Sho did," George said with satisfaction.

"Good boys. Fust day we can take off from the field work, we'll go rob it."

When that day came the swamp was dry enough for us to take the wagon. Daddy Floyd loaded in a two-man cross-cut saw, axes, wedges, maul, tubs and plenty of buckets. It was almost like a picnic. Everybody in the Snowden and Floyd families went along to help bring back the bounty.

When we left the road, I walked ahead following the lick trail. Vernell drove the wagon, gee-hawing around big trees. When we got close to the bee tree, Daddy Floyd told Vernell to tie up the mules about fifty yards away. "Ah don't want a pair of bee-stung, crazy mules to teah up our wagon," he said. Years later, I heard a man in Missouri use the expression, "crazy as a bee-stung mule," and I knew he was one of my Southern countrymen.

My uncles, Cecil and Vernell, grabbed the saw and cut a third of the way into the trunk, about three feet above the ground. They then sawed out a wedge of wood above the first cut, exposing the hollow core which ran all the way up to the bee hive. The vibrations from the sawing excited the bees but, fortunately, they didn't associate it with us.

Daddy Floyd and George's father built a dry wood fire at the base of the tree under the notched hole. They added green leaves to make the fire smoke. The smoke coursed up the hollow and came out the hole where the bees had flown into the hive. The bees came pouring out.

"Cut 'er down, boys," Daddy Floyd ordered.

My uncles sawed as fast as they could. The tree fell with a thunderous crash that echoed through the thick woods.

Knowing the bees would soon be returning, the men started another smoke fire on the windward side of the bee hole. Smoke from that fire kept drifting across the hive entrance while Vernell and Cecil cut through the trunk just above the hole. Then they sawed completely through the trunk about four feet below the bee opening. That gave us a four-foot section of trunk packed with honey.

Daddy Floyd hit the hive section with an ax to start the split. He drove in steel wedges with a maul and in short order split the trunk into two halves, exposing the hive of raw, yellow honey.

Grandmother and Mrs. Snowden sliced up the hive while Daddy Floyd and Mr. Snowden filled up the buckets with the pieces. Helen Maude, Doris, George and I stayed busy emptying buckets into the tubs and passing back empties to the men.

Finally, when my arms were about given out, Daddy Floyd announced, "Folks, that's enough. Let's leave some foah the bees to make it through the winter." We all knew that once the hive had been "robbed," the bees would start a new hive in safer territory.

We loaded the tools and tubs full of honey into the wagon for the trip back. The Snowdens took their tub home and we carried ours into the house where I joined the women folk in separating the honey from the comb. While we worked there, Daddy Floyd, Vernell and Cecil cleaned out the wagon and unhitched and fed the mules.

My crew drained the honey combs through a screen into another tub. The combs would later be warmed for the final extraction of any remaining honey.

We dipped the strained honey into small containers to warm slowly on the kitchen stove. Then it was strained through cheesecloth two more times and put in storage containers.

Finally, the drained combs were heated till they liquified, then poured into pans to cool. We cut the resulting wax into fudge-like cubes. The wax would later be used to make candles, leather preservative, shoe waterproofer, twine, rope strengthener and for many other uses.

Many hands made work light and we finished in a short afternoon. Grandmother's biscuits now baked in the oven.

When the biscuits were done, she called, "Come an' enjoy." We clambered onto the benches at the kitchen table and Grandmother placed pans of fluffy, piping hot biscuits before our hungry eyes.

Daddy Floyd led us in a prayer of thanksgiving. Doris and Helen Maude passed the plates and forks. Cecil and Vernell showed us how real men mounded country butter and ladled fresh, wild honey on their biscuits. As we all took our first bites, Cecil called out, "Hoo, Lawd! What a time an' place t'be livin'!"

And we all said, "Amen."

George and his parents came over a little later. Cecil and Vernell left for a party with their friends. Daddy Floyd, Grandmother and Mrs. Snowden reclined on the porch while George and I chased lightning bugs with Doris and Helen Maude.

After awhile, George's mother " 'lowed" they'd "bettah be gettin' along home."

"I'll be over in the mawnin'," George assured me. "We'll go find a new pool of fish and maybe another honey tree."

I went to bed feeling that with a friend like George, life was almost perfect. I say "almost" because Mother wasn't with me and I wouldn't be seeing her again for at least two months.

Chapter 11

"Uncle Semmy and His Front Stuffer"

My older cousin Vena Mae had forgotten to tell me something. Aunt Maggie or Uncle Ban must have reminded her because their mule-drawn wagon stopped out beyond our barn and Vena Mae came running back all out of breath.

She spoke in her soft southern drawl. "Pa says if yuh really wanta' learn howta' fish, then come ovah tomorrah aftahnoon an' Uncle Semmy can teach yuh."

By the time I had absorbed the invitation and called out, "Who's Uncle Semmy?" my skinny second cousin had clambered over the tail gate of the wagon and my question was drowned out by Uncle Ban shouting, "Giddap, mules!"

I could have run down alongside the wagon to request more information, but Uncle Ban had always intimidated me. Not that he had ever been mean. But with his stern face, one glance could freeze my laughter in mid-air. I don't remember him ever smiling at me or anyone else.

Uncle Ban was small and bow-legged — "from ridin' hosses so much when he was a youngun," Aunt Maggie always said. Standing five feet five and with arms hanging out from his sides, he was not a handsome sight. His crumpled felt hat was his constant companion winter or summer. He was a good farmer, working long, hard hours in the fields. "The groun' don't daah withhol' from 'im," Aunt Maggie said with a twinkle in her eye.

Aunt Maggie was small in stature like Uncle Ban but there the likeness ended. She was always happy with a merry wide mouth that smiled even when she wasn't trying. I knew she really cared what I thought because she never talked at me, she talked to me.

That day I turned to go in our house with a dozen unspoken questions in my mind.

Why do they think Ah don't know how to fish? Ah've been catchin' fish with George Snowden foah two years.

Who's this Uncle Semmy an' wheah's he live? Is he married? does he have any chirrun? Wheah'd he come from?

I poured out my questions to Grandmother and Daddy Floyd at the supper table.

"Ah nevah heard of him. Did you, Floyd?"

"No, can't say Ah evah did, Jennie."

Despite my foreboding, I was intrigued. It might be fun to learn some new fishing tricks, I decided. Show ole George Snowden that I was more grown-up than some people took me to be.

I looked from Daddy Floyd to Grandmother. "Is it awl right if Ah go see this Uncle Semmy?"

Grandmother frowned. "Ah don't like you messin' with strangahs we haven't met."

Daddy Floyd tapped her on the wrist. "Aw, Jennie, youah sistah and brothah-in-law must think he's all right or they wouldn't have invited Jimmie to come." My grandfather tossed me a reassuring smile. "Go on ovah theah tomorrow, boy. Make an adventure out of it."

When you're almost ten, everything is now. Later is years away. So I waited impatiently until noon the following day. At precisely twelve-o-one p.m. I strolled on to Aunt Maggie and Uncle Ban's front porch. Trying to appear nonchalant I tapped on the front door. Vena Mae answered my knock wearing an apron over her blue print house dress.

"Hey, Jimmie. Whatcha doin' ovah heah?"

"Hey, Vena Mae. Ah came ovah to see 'bout that 'Uncle' Semmy."

"Well, he's not heah," she drawled, "He's down at the fish camp. That's wheah he's been livin', all by his lonesome." She turned down the hall and I followed her to the kitchen.

"Hey, Jimmie," smiled Aunt Maggie. "Want some dinnah?" She leaned over as I presented my cheek for the ritual relative kiss.

"No ma'am, Ah've had dinnah. Ah jus came ovah 'bout that Mistuh, uh 'Uncle' Semmy." I was trying not to let my excitement show.

"Wael, he's down at the fish camp, so yuh jus' go on down," Aunt Maggie urged.

My heart beat increased at the thought of meeting a mysterious stranger all alone. But I felt it would be all right if Aunt Maggie sent me. Even if Uncle Ban wasn't home.

"Tell 'im 'Hey' for me, will yuh Jimmie?", Aunt Maggie called as I crossed the backyard.

"Yessum, Ah will," I answered over my shoulder.

I noticed Brutus, Uncle Ban's menacing black bull standing sullenly in the barn lot, so I circled around and climbed through the fence at the bottom of the hill to cross the pasture. Usually, I cut through Uncle Ban's barn lot to reach the pasture but I didn't want any "truck" with Brutus today.

I carried my special fishing pole, a slender, swamp grown, smooth bark hickory. In the other hand I clutched a can of fresh, fat worms, dug up from around the edges of the manure pile back at Daddy Floyd's barn. I hoped the bait would impress this mysterious Uncle Semmy.

The fish camp was a cabin that perched beside a little lake at the far south edge of Uncle Ban's pasture, about 200 feet from Chunky River. The cabin was a plain clapboard structure about thirty feet long with shutters running the full length on both sides. At mid-day a thick grove of water oaks completely shaded the house and grounds.

Approaching ever more slowly, I swallowed and re-swallowed the same lump in my throat with each step. It didn't improve my nervousness even somewhat to hear the wind eerily moaning through the trees. The solid, dark gray cabin had a foreboding appearance. I tried to whistle so as not to surprise him. But my whistle was too dry and I couldn't get my pucker shaped just right.

Rounding the corner of the cabin I approached the only door and called timidly, "Mistuh Semmy?".

I noticed my voice had a queer crackle to it.

No answer.

"Mistuh Semmy?".

No answer.

I felt a rising desire to be somewhere else.

Suddenly, the door jerked open and a bearded, one-armed apparition stood in the frame.

"Who' ah yuh boy?"

"Mah name's Jimmie Rogers an' mah Uncle Ban said yuh might teach me how to fish if yuh had a mind to an' if Ah didden get in yoah way an' cause yuh any trouble."

Without a word, he held up a hand for silence. Staring at me for a long minute, he mumbled, "Ah swan, boy, yuh sho' do run off at t'mouth."

He looked me up and down very carefully, then said, "Tarn 'roun, boy."

As my back was turned I heard him say softly, "He sho' is puny, Edith, but mehbe he'll do."

I whirled back around to see this mysterious Edith, but we were alone. After what seemed like a long time he made his decision.

"Wael, yuh kin come 'roun but yuh got t'do whut Ah sez. Yuh walk sof' an' yuh don't make me tell you sumthin' twicet'. Iffen Ah tell yuh 'stop,' you bettah stop, or you'ah lackely goin' t'step on a cottonmout' moccasin. Yuh call me Uncle Semmy an' don't yuh nevah ask me no dumb questions."

As he gave his orders I was transfixed by his piercing eyes. I said it instantly: "Yassuh."

"Wait heah, boy." He retreated into the cabin and while he was gone I reflected on what I'd seen. To say his appearance was scary was an understatement. He was skinny to the point of boniness. His unkempt hair covered his ears and had obviously never been close to a comb. His weather-worn face was road mapped by the spoilation of time. A short growth of hair covered his face, not a real beard, but more like he hadn't shaved for a couple of weeks.

His right arm was missing, gone all the way to the shoulder. Not even a stump remained. He wore a raggedy pair of overalls and long cotton underwear, even in the heat of summer. His right underwear sleeve was pinned neatly across his chest. He was as barefooted as a pup.

After awhile he stepped out the door and without a word picked up a cane pole leaning against the side of the cabin. Retrieving a can from under the shade of the wooden steps, he headed for Chunky River. I dutifully followed behind.

His gait was strange, more like gliding than walking. The balls of his bare feet hit the ground before his heels—just like the Indians walked. I tried to imitate his walk but I gave it up because it felt so awkward. We reached the river bank and he squatted down on a shaded sandbar to bait his hook.

I proudly dumped over my can of worms, my big beauties. "Yuh want one of these?" I asked, trying to sound casual.

He shook his head and dumped his own can over.

My eyes bugged at his "gran'daddy" worms.

"Them's night crawlahs," Uncle Semmy announced, "Ah gettum in youah Uncle Ban's paschah aftah dahk."

I wondered how he was going to bait a hook with only one arm. I shouldn't have doubted. Before I could start stringin' a big wiggler on my own hook, he had put the night crawler down under the big toe of his right foot and skillfully impaled it with the hook.

So my newest fishing lessons began.

I learned how a big bass could be caught by pulling a night crawler along the bottom, drawing the bait slowly toward you with the line held lightly between your thumb and forefinger. "When the bass strikes," Uncle Semmy noted, "he'll pluck the line from youah fingers an' staht swimmin' away. Jus' let 'im run with it," he continued, as he reached out over the water with his pole, giving the fish that had taken his bait plenty of slack.

"One, two, three, foah, five, six," he counted — mostly for my benefit, I thought.

Then while I excitedly hopped from one foot to the other he slowly pulled in the slack and with a sharp snap of the pole set the hook. I was dumbfounded at the lunker he pulled out of the water! I had no idea there were fish that big in Chunky River. Oh, sure, catfish but not bass.

Uncle Semmy also taught me how to toss a small leaf in the water and watch as the current swept it into an eddy by an old log lying in the water. "Food goes t'same place as leaves," he observed.

In another lesson I learned that fish congregate in "schools" under logs in the water and that I could catch six or eight at one spot until they quit biting. Then five or ten feet farther down the log I could find another school.

He showed me how to pull up my bait if a fish didn't bite and let it plop back in the water. "Iffen a bug falls in the watah it makes a liddle splash an' sends out ripples," he mused, like he was talking to himself. "An ole hongry bass will come runnin'."

He taught me how to hook "uncatchable" bream. These fish were so well disguised you could look directly at them through five inches of clear water over their hollowed bed of twigs and leaves and never see them. If you dangled a worm on a hook in their nest it simply disappeared before your very eyes, with never the slightest twitch. So it had been for me before Uncle Semmy.

On a later adventure, Uncle Semmy observed me feeding the bream one day in the lake near the cabin. He watched silently while I lost my bait three times in a row. Then he trudged forward and took the pole from my hands.

"Heah, lak' this." Rebaiting the hook, he draped the line over a slender twig that extended over the nest, and dangled the bait about an inch from the bottom. The twig twitched ever so slightly and with a deft snap he flipped the bream out on the bank.

"Don't look at nuthin' but the twig, boy," he drawled, completing that lesson.

Hand fishing became a new thrill for me but I was taught that if my hand ever encountered air in a hole in the bank or a hollow log in the stream I was to pull it out quick. "Cottonmout' moccasins live in them kinds of holes," Uncle Semmy warned.

Hand fishing is illegal nowadays, but this was a good part of Uncle Semmy's livelihood. In 1934 nobody had a job for a one-armed man who had never been to school.

Not that he was illiterate. One evening I was leaving the camp when he said, "Boy, does youah gran'folks happen to get a newspapuh?"

"Yessuh, the mailman brings them the **Meridian Star**."

"An' whut do they do with the papuh when they'ah through?"

I suppressed a giggle. "It goes to the outhouse."

"Uh, huh. Do yuh suppose it would be a bothah foah them to let me have the front part when theah're through? 'Fo they take it to the outhouse."

"Ah'll ask 'um," I promised.

Almost every day except Sunday, for the rest of that marvelous summer, I brought the paper. It was the least I could do for what he was teaching me.

He read only the front page and the editorials, sometimes nodding, sometimes shaking his head. "These ah hahd times," I heard him say more than once. "Ah figguh a man kin allus do sumthin' t'arn a livin' an' thim as works hahd kin live bettah."

Uncle Semmy was a subsistence fisherman, hunter and trapper. What he did wasn't fancy or even sporting, it was just effective. He taught me how to take a hoe and "muddy" the water-filled depressions left in the woods when the river receded within its banks. When the fish brought their mouths close to the surface to suck in the relatively clear water, he splashed them out on the bank by striking the water with the heel of his hoe just in front of them. George Snowden and I had almost stumbled on the way to do this the past summer, but we were trying to rake the fish out instead of splashing them out.

Uncle Semmy used every trick in his bag to catch fish, but he absolutely refused to "buckeye" a lake because even the little fish would be poisoned. "God don't lak' us to waste," he declared.

Even crusty old hard shell mussels on the bottom of Chunky River have a soft interior and so did Uncle Semmy. I never visited his cabin that golden summer without seeing freshly cut wild flowers gracing old jelly jars on his table or window sills.

His floral arrangements varied by the season. Once he even made a bouquet of bitterweed. My favorite flowers were the delicate white and pink Cherokee rose and the giant, almost sickening sweet, blossoms of the magnolia tree. Without him asking, I climbed the huge magnolias leaning over the river and gathered blossoms for him and Grandmother. One-armed men don't climb trees.

Once he saw me admiring his flowers in their jelly jars and he touched each one gently in their turn and quietly spoke their names. Occasionally, I asked him the name of something in the woods but only after weighing the words carefully in my mind to be sure I wasn't asking a "dumb" question. Now and then I brought him crepe myrtle, wisteria or roses from Grandmother's flower garden and placed them in his gnarled left hand. Somehow the flowers seemed to smooth out the time-worn calluses and seams in his skin.

My tenth birthday came and went. School started back about a month later and we were into September when Mother got a few days off from work and paid a surprise visit. That Saturday evening I saw her smiling as she rocked on the porch with Daddy Floyd and Grandmother while Doris and I played in the yard.

Later in the evening, Grandmother announced that it was bedtime for Doris and me. I slipped out of my cutoffs and got into the little narrow bed where I slept in the boys' bedroom.

The buzz of women's voices on the porch kept me awake. Finally I pulled my clothes back on and tiptoed into the hall to hear. They were talking about me.

"Oh, Mothah," I heard her say to Grandmother in her mixture of Northern and Southern brogues, "I'd give anything if I could take mah dahlin' boy back to St. Louis with me."

"Ah know that, Ruth. It's only natural foah a mother to love her child."

"I don't know what I'd do without you and Daddy. You care for Jimmie like he was your own child."

"He's our grandson and you're our daughter. That's what a family is for."

"Well, I keep lookin' for a good husband. One who will love me and be a good father to Jimmie.

One who will be loyal and faithful to me, not like that no good who left me."

Daddy Floyd called to Grandmother from their bedroom.

"Ah'm comin'," Grandmother answered.

I crept silently back down the hall and slipped into the boys' room. I stayed awake a long time thinking of what might change if Mother got married again.

All of Mother's visits were too brief and this was no exception. On Tuesday we took her to the station in Meridian where she hugged me tight and told me, "Some day I'm gonna marry a good man and bring you to live with us." Then she wiped away her tears, stepped on to the train, and was gone again.

I hadn't seen Uncle Semmy for at least two weeks when he sent word by Vena Mae for me to come over early the next Saturday with my rifle. By "early" I knew he meant before daylight.

On the appointed day Daddy Floyd prodded me out of bed before he went out to milk the cows and feed the animals. I found a kerosene lantern and purloined two big pieces of sizzling side meat bacon from Grandmother's iron skillet and placed them on two biscuits from yesterday's breakfast. I rolled them up in a newspaper with a big hunk of corn bread and two onions. A quart jar of buttermilk completed the lunch that I stuffed in an empty lard bucket. It was enough for two.

I carried my Stevens "Little Scout," the .22 rifle I had bought the year before by working as a water boy in Mr. Hopkins' cotton fields. The rifle cost three dollars and seventy-five cents, brand new, more than a half a week's wages. I could drive nail heads into a tree at ten paces.

It was too dark to take the shortcut through the fields and woods, so I hastened the long way up Okahatta Road to Sixteenth Road and hurried across the pasture down to the little cabin on the lake. As I trotted through the dewy grass I noticed the tinge of light in the east.

A lantern was shining outside the cabin and I braced myself for the certain criticism. It came swiftly from the deep stern voice in the dark.

"You'ah late, boy. Ah bin waitin' a long time."

I lamely answered, "Ah'm sorry."

That was all I dared say because Uncle Semmy didn't cotton to excuses.

"Yuh gotta do bettah."

Two sentences in a row meant that he was real aggravated.

"Yessuh, I will." And I really meant it.

He carried his lantern into the cabin. "C'mon, boy".

I watched as he set the lantern on the plain, clean kitchen table next to his opened Bible. A fire burned in his kitchen stove and I stepped near the welcome warmth. Even in Mississippi some October mornings are brisk. I waited as he stepped into his bedroom and returned with his gun.

"Ah'm gonna show yuh how to load a front stuffer," he announced.

Uncle Semmy carried the oldest gun I had ever seen but it looked brand spanking new. The stock and barrel gleamed from fresh polish and it had that nice sweet smell of gun oil. He placed the gun butt on the floor and curled his leg around it to hold the stock steady against his body. Holding an ancient powder horn with gleaming brass fittings, he poured a measure of powder down the barrel. Then he stretched a small swatch of striped cloth across the end of the barrel.

He next placed a marble-sized ball of lead on top of the cloth. Laying a wooden block with a depression in it on top of the ball, he struck the block smartly with the heel of his hand. The lead ball seated just below the center line in the barrel with the cloth curled up around the ball.

"Yuh payin' 'tention, boy?" he asked.

I nodded.

He took out his Case pocket knife and deftly trimmed away the excess cloth. "Allus use cotton," he mumbled. Removing the ramrod from its position under the barrel he placed it on top of the ball and rammed it home. "We'ah now ready to go huntin'." He struck out through the woods, with me trailing after.

We'd walked about a quarter of a mile when he stopped under a scaly-bark hickory tree and bent to pocket some nuts. I did too, not knowing why. He walked on a ways — perhaps another quarter — and stopped under a smaller tree.

"Sign," he said, nodding at the broken hickory nut shells on the ground under this tree.

He nodded toward another tree, about twenty yards away. Instinctively I slipped quietly over to that scaly-bark and turned to watch Uncle Semmy remove a handful of nuts from his pocket. I did the same at my tree.

He squatted under his tree and leaned back against it. I did the same at my position.

All this without an eye blink.

After a few minutes the woods started coming to life. Birds began their morning song; a raccoon scurried across the leaf-strewn woods' floor. A black snake took a brief look at me from about five feet away. I didn't move, didn't even blink, but he knew where I was and how big I was. Daddy Floyd had taught me that snakes can tell where you are by sensing your body temperature through their tongues. After a while the reptile apparently decided I was too big to eat and slithered away.

A quarter hour or more passed. I noticed Uncle Semmy looking at me. As soon as he saw me watching he tilted his head slowly back. He looked up the tree and ever so slightly lifted the end of his antique rifle. Lifting my .22 slowly so it pointed up the tree, I looked questioningly at him.

He silently nodded, and as I watched he threw a couple of hickory nuts on a high arc to the far side of the tree. Seizing his rifle, which had been leaning against his chest, he quickly raised it. The nuts crackled in the ground leaves when they fell. High up in the tree two squirrels skittered around the trunk to our side and hung there. Two shots rang out in unison and both squirrels dropped! I can still feel the thrill of that moment. It wasn't just shooting them, it was tracking, outwitting and outwaiting them that made it so exciting. A hunter was born!

Uncle Semmy shot five more squirrels that morning and I added two to my bag. We left the woods by nine a.m. and he skinned and dressed them all with his Case pocket knife.

He kept two squirrels for his own table and sent four by me to Aunt Maggie. The hides were set aside to be put on stretcher boards later. I proudly carried the other three squirrels home and Grandmother put them in salted water for dinner the next day.

The next Saturday Uncle Semmy introduced me to tracking. Uncle Ban's cows had scattered through the woods, and Uncle Semmy found them in a half hour. A bent over branch of a bush, a broken swamp palmetto leaf blade, even the angry chatter of disturbed squirrels, were as clear to him as written directions.

Once he stopped and pointed to a hoof imperfection imprinted in a track and muttered, "Thet's the ole brown un'." Again he noted a track that indicated a slight drag when the hoof came forward. "The black an' white 'un."

I shook my head in amazement.

Later we were coming out of the woods into the pasture when out jumped a rabbit.

Instantly Uncle Semmy began a rolling, repetitive whistle. The rabbit stopped almost at once! A quick shot and the hare was ready for Uncle Semmy's larder. "Koorosity kills moah'n cats," was his terse comment.

Years later, on a summer vacation, I was in Daddy Floyd's pasture without a rifle and demonstrated Uncle Semmy's technique to my family. Walking softly while I whistled, I was leaning over to grab the rabbit with my hands before he finally broke and ran. I had often wondered how close I could get.

Memories of dear Uncle Semmy still whistle through the recesses of my mind. Far too many to recount here. I learned over time that he had been in World War I and had been gassed. He had married, settled near New Orleans and had lost his arm to a monster gar in the Mississippi, downriver from New Orleans. He'd pulled the huge fish into his boat. As he leaned over to reach his oars, the gar lunged up and bit him savagely in the upper arm, ripping the ligaments and the muscle and blood vessels apart.

It must have required a superhuman effort to get his boat to shore using an oar as a paddle, after winding a makeshift tourniquet around his useless arm. That explained his actions the day I watched him savagely beat a gar to death that he'd pulled from Chunky River.

Much of what I learned about Uncle Semmy came from Uncle Ban through Aunt Maggie, but I never discovered who Edith was that he talked to now and then. She may have been his long dead wife. I never told a living soul about hearing him call her name, and I pretended not to hear him. I feared people would mistake terrible loneliness and a lost love for being "teched in the haid." I later speculated that he had come by the name "Semmy" as a contraction of Seminole. Uncle Ban said Uncle Semmy was raised by an Indian family and perhaps that family had been Seminole.

Uncle Ban and Aunt Maggie could not have chosen a better outdoors' teacher for me than Uncle Semmy. He didn't smoke, chew tobacco, drink alcohol, use profanity or ever talk obscenely about women. He was a man who had been terribly abused by life, so he simply dropped out and went to live where he could no longer be hurt.

The day came when I went over to fish with my friend and Aunt Maggie called me into the house. She wasn't smiling now and was so distraught that the ritual greeting kiss was forgotten. I'd never seen her so sad before.

Folding me in her arms, she said, "He's gone, Jimmie."

She released me, but seeing my uncomprehending eyes and my frozen smile, she repeated, "Uncle Semmy left; he had to go away, but he said to give you this."

She placed in my hand his treasured Case pocket knife — the knife which he had used to skin the squirrels on our first hunting trip together.

My eyes instantly brimmed full and in my grief I threw the pocket knife to the floor, fled from the house and down the road. From behind I heard Uncle Ban's voice.

"Come back, Vena Mae, let 'im be."

Wise Uncle Ban.

There are times when you must be alone to face your heartbreak. I walked in the deep woods for hours. Then I went home and cried out my remaining tears on Grandmother's lap.

Later I went back to retrieve the knife from Aunt Maggie. "No, we've not heard nuthin' from Uncle Semmy," she said.

Over six decades the memories remain fresh of this dear man who taught me the skills of surviving in the woods and swamp. I expect to see him again in that treasured beyond where I hope God will provide us with a river and woods.

Chapter 12

"Brothah and Nell"

My oldest uncle — Cecil Howard — was 18 years older than I. His accent was much, much broader than the other members of the family. I loved to hear him drawl in his deep mellow voice, "Jimmie, come heah, Ah've got somethin' foah yuh."

From my earliest remembrance I called him "Brothah."

Brothah — Cecil — worked for the Newton County Road Department in a two man road grading crew. He usually drove the Caterpillar tractor that pulled the grader but sometimes he switched and operated the grader. He and his partner graded one side of the road for half the day and then turned around and graded the other side during the afternoon.

Grandmother allowed me and my sidekick, Sport, to go meet Brothah on the road that ran through the Okahatta Swamp when his ten-hour work day was over. I was only about six years old when I started doing this but across the years I can still remember the excitement I felt when I rounded a bend and saw my big Brothah.

He always saved a bit of his lunch for me, usually a bacon biscuit. I rode on his shoulders home happily eating my reward as Sport bounced around his feet barking in excitement. I dearly loved Brothah.

Once when I was about eight I heard the sound of the Caterpillar as the road crew worked on the Okahatta Road down in the swamp. It was just before noon and, knowing that Brothah always stopped at exactly twelve noon to eat, I grabbed up a couple of leftover breakfast biscuits, picked two big tomatoes from the garden and ran down the road to eat with him. After we ate he asked, "Would you like to drive the Cat, Jimmie?"

Would I? I nodded my head vigorously.

He unhooked the grader and sat me on his lap. He showed me how to pull the brake levers and he used the clutch pedals for me.

"Heah we go! Hang on, Jimmie."

I rumbled across the ditch and into the woods, knocking down small trees and clearing a path through underbrush. "Rhummmmm, rhummmmmm!" I growled.

Brothah let me go with it. "Atta boy, Jimmie. Yuh really know how to handle this ole Cat."

A big oak loomed in my path. Brothah grabbed the right brake lever just in time.

Around and around, backwards and forwards, I took the Caterpillar with my uncle keeping a sharp eye out for trees I couldn't push over. My chest pushed my overalls out. "Wheee! Wheee!"

Brothah seemed to be enjoying the ride as much as I. But all good things have to end sometime, and he braked the big machine to a stop.

I ran into school the next morning and proudly announced, "Ah drove a Caterpillar!" For the rest of the week I was the envy of all the boys until Otho Harris brought a big hornets' nest to school. It was as big around as a basketball. My Cat story was an instant has-been. Otho took his hornets' nest to the hardware store and they placed it in the store window with a sign that said, "Loaned by Otho Harris." I wished I could put a sign in the window that said, "Jimmie Rogers is a Caterpillar driver."

Brothah was one of the best horsemen in the county and I loved to see him ride. In later years he owned a Tennessee Walking Horse and what a magnificent brute that horse was! He stood sixteen hands tall with a proud arched neck and long sweeping tail. Brothah was a Mason then and rode in parades all over the state. He loved that horse like he could have loved a son and wouldn't let anybody else ride him. Once he offered to let me ride him but I knew how he felt about his horse, so I declined. He seemed relieved.

Brothah liked to tell big whoppers, particularly to me, and he always hooked me real good. Like the time I caught a big grinnell and brought it up to the house to show everybody. A grinnell is a prehistoric fish that's just bones, tough scaly hide and meanness. Grinnels taste like mud and nobody eats them.

If one gets out of a main stream during a flood and can't get back when the floodwaters recede, it stays in a swamp pool until the water evaporates. Then it wiggles down into the mud and hibernates until the next flood, when it squirms out again.

When Brothah came home from work, I held my grinnel proudly out to him. He pretended to be impressed. Then without telling him I threw it out to the cats.

After Brothah got cleaned up he came out on the porch where I was sitting. "Jimmie, go getch'u fish an' Ah'll hep yuh fix it foah cookin'."

I should have known better but I took the bait right off. I said, "Ah gave 'im to the cats; sides, grinnells ahn't good to eat, Brothah."

"Whatchu' mean, Jimmie? Grinnells ah neah'bout the bes' thing goin' if yuh fix 'um propah'."

"How's that?" I said, still helping him set the hook. He sat down on the back porch steps to put on clean socks as he spun his web.

"Wael yuh staht a fiah in a liddle ole hole in the groun' an' while it's burnin' down to coals yuh go down to the woods an' climb way up a tree an' gitcha some muscadine leaves. Yuh bring back the leaves an' yuh rub that ole fish down with buttah an' sprinkle salt an' peppah on 'im. Nex' yuh slice some onion on 'im an' wrap the whole mess up in leaves, an' pack it awl in mud. Yuh plop that ole fish on top o' youah coals an' covah 'im with dirt."

"But Brothah — "

He held up his hand. "Now wait a minnit 'an lissen, Jimmie. Afta' 'bout 'n houah yuh dig up that ole fish', an yuh unwrap 'im an' yuh throw away the fish an' eat the mud an' muscadine leaves."

For a long time I just stood there trying to comprehend what had happened, and then I spoke—but nobody heard me. While Brothah was spinning his story everybody had gathered around to listen—and did they laugh. At me!

I turned red and began sputtering. Brothah grabbed me and threw me up in the air almost into the limbs of the chinaberry tree. He caught me coming down and started tickling my ribs. How could I stay mad at him now? Besides, I was already planning how I was going to get Ray McGee on the joke next Saturday afternoon when we went to town.

There was a story about Brothah that went untold for years and years after it happened. It wasn't one bit funny to Grandmother and Daddy Floyd when it took place.

Brothah rode ole Jude, Daddy Floyd's biggest mule, to Hickory when he was eighteen to meet a couple of friends. They met up with a new boy from Chunky. "Hey, Ah got some white lightnin' in a jug," he said. "Yuh fellahs wanna sample it?"

Brothah's two pals and the Chunky boy took swigs, but Brothah declined. "Ah wouldn't care foah any," he kept saying, meaning that he didn't want to disgrace his daddy and mother.

"Aw, come on, Cecil. Come on, boy. One little swallah won't hurt yuh." They kept this up until he finally gave in. He gulped one drink and smacked his lips. "Ah think Ah'll have anothah, if yuh don't mind." He took another and another and another, until he was wobbling like Dr. Gilmore. Then he began singing and yodeling ala Jimmie Rodgers, the blues singer.

"How ah we gonna get him home?" Alvin Brown wondered. "He cain't ride the mule by hisself."

"Throw 'im in the back of mah pickup an' we'll drop 'im off," Oscar Williams proposed.

After positioning Brothah in the truck bed, the other three climbed in the cab. Brothah kept singing.

They were on the Okahatta Creek Bridge when Alvin asked, "Whatta'ya think Mr. James is goin' to do when he sees ole Cecil drunker than a hoot owl? He might come out with his shotgun. Ah heah he's a purty good shot."

Suddenly Brothah's bender wasn't funny after all.

"Ah'll drive by the house real fast and check things out," Oscar proposed.

Brothah didn't cooperate. Just as they whizzed past the house, he let out a loud yodel from the truck bed. That was not a sound Daddy Floyd heard every night at two-thirty in the morning.

Oscar turned around at the north sharecrop house, slowing long enough for Alvin to climb in back and clap his hand over Brothah's mouth. They drove back without lights, coasting to a stop with the engine turned off. They deposited Brothah in the front yard, whirled around, and blazed back down the hill, listening to the fading refrains of Brothah warbling, "Sweet Georgia Brown."

Daddy Floyd came stomping out of the house, followed by Grandmother wiping her eyes. "Whatevah is goin' on out heah?" she asked.

He pointed to the form that was Brothah, still singing at the top of his lungs. "This, Jennie, is what's goin' on. Cecil Howard. Our oldest son. Dog drunk."

Daddy Floyd and Grandmother dragged Brothah around to the back porch and poured cold well water over his head, until he at least stopped singing.

Then Daddy Floyd asked him, "Cecil, wheah is the mule?"

"Pappa, wheah IS that mule?" In his drunken stupor, Brothah kept repeating that question over and over, each time accenting a different word. "Pappa, WHEAH is that mule? Pappa, wheah is THAT mule? Pappa, wheah is that MULE?"

About the fifth time around, Daddy Floyd gave up. "Thunderation! Ah'll have to go find that mule myself. Put Cecil to bed, Jennie."

Daddy Floyd walked the three miles into Hickory, found his mule standing sound asleep, tied up at the town square, and rode him home.

The event was too embarrassing to discuss for a long time. Years later it became a funny story, even to my God-fearing grandparents.

Meanwhile, Brothah got a well-paying mechanic job in Jackson, the state capital, at a shop that sold and serviced heavy duty equipment. He met his first big challenge in trying to recover a huge drag line that drowned out while crossing a rising creek. Within a few hours the water had completely covered the cab and only the boom stuck above water.

Brothah's shop superintendent proposed trucking in two big bulldozers with giant cables to haul out the drag line and pull it on to the flat bed of a big truck. The truck driver would then transport the drag line a hundred miles to Jackson for dry out and repair. Then it would be returned to the job site.

Brothah boldly disagreed. "Ah don't think that'll do it. It'll take a bunch of men and equipment."

Brothah's alternate plan would only cost one tenth as much. At first the shop super laughed at the idea, but Brothah stuck to his guns and a loud argument resulted.

The owner came running out from his office, asking, "What's going on between you two?"

"Looks as if we've got different ideas on how to get the drag line out," Brothah said.

The owner listened to both plans and to the shop super's surprise, said, "Let's go with Cecil's."

Brothah loaded three scoop shovels, 300 cloth bags and a gasoline powered generator and pump on a pickup truck. Taking along two mechanics, he headed for the site about thirty miles south of Hickory, stopping on the way to buy ten ordinary hair dryers and then to pick me up on the road. "Bring youah swim suit, Jimmie," Brothah said. He drove on, the mechanics riding in the truck cab with Brothah, and me perched on top of the boxes of bags having a great time.

When we reached the site, Brothah told us to put on our swim suits and start shoveling sand into the bags. "We'ah gonna build a three-sided coffahdam wall 'round the drag line," Brothah declared.

One of the mechanics put down his shovel and looked at Brothah in amazement. "Cecil, you've sho gone aroun' the bend this time. You'ah the craziest man in Dixie an' that's sayin' sumthin.' "

But, funny thing, as the work progressed the men slowly began to believe in the plan. They pumped out the water inside the cofferdam and dried out the electrical gear on the drag line. The diesel engine was cleaned, re-oiled and started to the cheers of the two men and myself. Brothah then pulled the drag line out of the creek under its own power.

Brothah dropped me at the farm and returned to Jackson, only to find his tools and the contents of his locker stacked on the loading dock with a pink termination notice on top. Brothah didn't say a word or get mad. He just started loading up his things on his pickup to leave.

"Hey! Hold up!"

Brothah turned to see his two helpers and the shop owner coming toward him. The next day the sign on the office read, "Cecil James, Shop Superintendent."

I was always proud to call him, "Brothah."

Luther Vernell was my youngest uncle. He went by "Vernell," but as a toddler I got to calling him "Nell" and that sort of stuck for me. Nell was fifteen years older than I and different from Brothah in that he looked on me with a kind of amused tolerance.

Brothah might have been the best horse rider, but nobody in the county could beat Nell when it came to handling a team of horses or mules in the field.

Nell actually liked to plow with the big twelve-inch turning plow used to clear new ground and make terraces. It took two mules to pull one of Daddy Floyd's man-breaking middle-busters. After a man piloted one of these plows all day, he looked like he'd "been rode hard an' put away wet."

Even Daddy Floyd's biggest mule, Ole Jude couldn't pull a turning plow alone. The offspring of a Percheron mare and a donkey stud, Jude had only two speeds according to Daddy Floyd: "dead slow an' dead," but boy, could that mule pull! And Nell was strong as an ox and could wrestle a team pulling a turning plow, and still be ready to go places at the end of a day.

Once Nell was driving us in the wagon to town to see Mother at her little restaurant. I was only three, going on four, since Mother hadn't given up the business yet. Days and days of rain had pushed Okahatta Creek out of its banks and flood waters covered the road, making it impossible to get through with a car.

Brothah was hollering at the team to "move it," when I asked Daddy Floyd, "Can Ah stand up in front to watch the mules?"

"Well, Ah reckon so, Jimmie. That dashboard oughta be high 'nough ta hold yuh in."

Daddy Floyd lifted me over the seat and put me down between Nell's legs. "Yuh hold on tight, boy, yuh heah?"

The mud was so deep that the wagon axles were dragging in the road bed. Brothah slapped the reins against the mules' rumps. "Come up mules! Pull! Move it!"

The road through the swamp had once been lined with logs to create a roadbed. Over the years these logs had been pushed deeper and deeper into the mud by traffic. Suddenly the wagon's front wheels dropped into a hole and struck one of the old logs. The wagon jolted to a jarring stop.

"Jimmie!"

Nell hollered too late. I flew up and over the dashboard toward the mules' flailing hind legs. Nell moved like lightening. He leaned forward and caught me in midair by the back of my overall straps and jerked me back against the outside of the dashboard. Pulling my right arm up and over, he clamped it against the dashboard with his knee.

"Somebody hold on to Jimmie," Nell hollered, as he fought the frenzied mules with both hands on the reins.

Daddy Floyd reached under Nell's arms, clapped me in a vise-like grip and pulled me back into the wagon. I sat trembling, my arm aching so bad I thought it had been jerked off.

"Come up mules!" Nell yelled, slashing them with the reins.

The mules heaved and strained against the harness. "Move it, you big boogers! Move it!" Nell hollered.

The wagon lurched forward in the floodwater. We were back in business.

When we reached town Doc Gilmore checked my arm. Other than being purple all the way up and sprained to boot, there was no lasting damage.

"Ah think he'll heal up an' live, Floyd," Doc told my grandfather. "Jus' keep 'im quiet foah awhile."

Thanks to Nell's quick thinking, I survived.

This wasn't the only time Nell came to my rescue. Several years after Brothah moved to Jackson, I was running my set lines in Okahatta Creek. I climbed over a big oak log and noticed one of my fishing poles had been pulled out of the bank.

I figured a turtle might have gotten hooked and pulled out the pole. Looking around I spotted the pole in an eddy a few yards downstream that swirled against a steep bank.

I broke off a sapling and raked the floating pole within reach. As I began pulling it in the pole almost bent double. Then it began moving.

I figured the line must have gotten snagged on an underwater log which the current was moving around. I pulled very slowly to avoid breaking the line.

Suddenly a dark shape appeared. The "log" had eyes and whiskers on a head the size of a milk bucket. My eyes bugging, I quickly wound the pole end of the line around a small bush.

No sooner had I done this than the monster specimen realized it was caught and began to thrash fiercely in the water. The bush bent sharply, then sprang back as the catfish frantically sought to throw the hook. I knew I couldn't pull that giant in. I raced toward the house and found Nell plowing in the field.

"Nell! Ah've got a cat on a setline biggah than a cow. So big Ah cain't pull it out!" My mouth was running a mile a minute.

"Whoa! Whoa!" He pulled the mules to a halt.

"Now, run that by me again, Jimmie."

"Ah've got a cat on mah line biggah than a calf. It's so big Ah cain't pull it out."

"Yuh want me to come an' hep?"

"Yeah, yeah. Ah wrapped mah line around a bush. Hurry, Nell 'fo it breaks the line."

Nell quickly tied up the mules and ran back with me to the creek.

"Theah! Theah!" I pointed at the bush that was alternately bending and snapping back.

Nell took the pole and expertly drew the fish closer. My eyes widened as I saw him reach his hand into the big cat's mouth and run his fingers out the gills.

Sharp teeth clamped around Nell's arm. The giant fish jerked and flopped, trying to break free. Nell's blood reddened the water.

"Stand back, Jimmie, Ah'm bringing it out." With that he dragged the fish onto the bank and held it up for me to see. It was longer than my legs!

All I could say was, "Whut a fish"!

He even carried it home for me. Grandmother and my aunts' eyes ran out on stems. Daddy Floyd heard the shouting and came running from the barn. "That," he said, "is what Ah'd call a big'un. Who caught it?"

Nell pointed to me. "Jimmie hooked it in the creek on one of his setlines."

I grinned at Nell, mumbling, "Nell helped get it out." I should have said, "Nell pulled it out." Nell didn't say a word.

Nell and Brothah both looked out for their little nephew.

Chapter 13

"The Wild Dog"

At four a.m. the cackling in the hen house woke me from a sound sleep. From the boys' bedroom across the hall, I heard Grandmother. "Floyd, that egg-suckin', wild dawg is back."

Then Daddy Floyd: "Ah'll get mah gun."

Arming himself, Daddy Floyd rushed down the hall and out the back door. Nightshirt flapping, I ran after him, clutching my own .22 rifle. A few minutes later we reported back to Grandmother: "Dad-blamed wild varmint got away again."

The "wild" dog that I visualized as big as a wolf, came slyly and often. Much too often. Daddy Floyd always heard the frantic cackling of the chickens in the hen house, signalling the thief's presence. But when he and I rushed out with our guns, the dog had fled in the warm night.

"We've got to get that animal 'fo he stahts killin' chickens," Daddy Floyd declared. "We" meant Daddy Floyd and his grandson, since Cecil and Vernell were working away from home.

"Heah's whut we'll do, Jimmie. Next time we heah that dog in the hen house, yuh run out in the front yahd an' Ah'll run in the back yahd an' flush the dawg under the house tow'd you. That way, maybe one uv us can get a clean shot at 'im."

We tried this on three different nights, but only once did Daddy Floyd get off a shot, and then he missed. I never got to pull my trigger once.

Then for a whole week the wild dog didn't come. "He'll be back," Daddy Floyd predicted. Ah'll keep an eah out an' when Ah yell, get yuh gun."

On a Saturday morning, about four a.m., the summons came. "He's heah again, Jimmie!"

Daddy Floyd's voice whispered in the silent blackness of that pre-dawn morning, but it carried an urgency that snapped me awake at once.

I spoke into the pale moonlight that filtered through a side window. "Ah'm goin' out the front door, Daddy Floyd."

I reached for my rifle that leaned against the wall across from my bed and sprinted down the hall and out the front door. I barely had time to position myself in the dirt road in front of the house when I heard Daddy Floyd's shout.

"He's a comin' undah the house right atcha, Jimmie!"

Standing in the wispy moonlight I braced myself, every sense alert. The invader lunged out of the inky shadows into the front yard. I fired one fast shot, almost in reflex, before stumbling backwards and falling in the dirt.

The marauder leaped over my body with a howl. Instinctively, I had drawn up my legs to protect my abdomen and had covered my face with crossed arms. I expected to feel the dog's sharp fangs slash into me at any instant but the attack never came.

I jumped to my feet and realized that my rifle had gone flying when I fell. Its single shot had been fired, but even an empty rifle had some value as a club. Quickly I scrambled to retrieve my gun and dashed to the safety of the front porch.

"Yeee, eeee, eeee." The yelps came from the corn field across the road and sounded like the dog was dying.

"Ah hit him, Daddy Floyd!"

"Yuh awl right, son?"

"Oh, Ah'm fine but he scahed me moah than somewhat."

"Yeee, eeee, eeee." The yelps came again.

Helen Maude called from behind the door screen. "Did yuh shoot the wild dog, Jimmie? He's makin' a powahful lot of noise out in the corn field"

My chest swelled with pride. "Yeah! Ah shot 'im, but he's so big it'd take moah than one shot to kill 'im. Ah 'speck he'll die quick from the bleedin' though."

My other aunt, Doris, showed me respect for a change. "Ah yuh goin' out to shoot 'im ag'in, Jimmie?"

Before I could reply, Grandmother's voice came out of the darkness. "No, Doris, Jimmie's not neah 'bout goin' to track that wounded animal in the moonlight."

I heaved a big sigh of relief at being ordered not to do what I was scared to do in the first place. Nevertheless I had to keep up a show of bravery. Doris would never let me live down any hint of cowardice.

"Ah wanna go after him, Grandmothah. Please, please," I begged, hoping she'd stick to her word.

"Now yuh can jus' quit that beggin', Jimmie. Youah mothah would nevah forgive me if Ah let yuh go out theah an' get bit by that wild animal. Yuh think that dog's mean? That's nothin' to what your mothah's goin' to be like if she comes an' finds out Ah let yuh get bit by a wild dawg."

I gasped when I heard Daddy Floyd speak. "Aw, Jennie, it would be good foah the boy to track the dog down — make a man out of 'im."

Could that have been a soft chuckle at the end of Daddy Floyd's sentence?

My voice swelled with pretended confidence. "Wael, Daddy Floyd, Ah reckon if Grandmothah is goin' tuh worry, maybe Ah'd bettah wait til sun-up."

I heard Daddy Floyd's laconic response. "Yeah, Ah 'speck yuh bettah."

The clock now read 4:25, only thirty-five minutes til wake-up time, so the family began getting ready for breakfast. Doris and Helen Maude asked me a lot of questions and I was happy to be the center of attention and answer them.

"How big was the wild dog, Jimmie?" asked Helen Maude.

"Ah 'speck he'd go 'bout eighty pounds, maybe even a hundred."

Daddy Floyd stood at the kitchen counter slicing bacon for Grandmother. In the light of the coal oil lamp, I saw his eyebrows arch.

"Did he act real mean?" Doris wondered.

"Yeh. I 'spect he's 'bout the meanest dog in Newton County. It wouldn't suhprise me none if he hadn't killed somebody, somewheah."

Helen Maude shivered and rose to pour Grandmother's bubbling hot chocolate. Throughout breakfast I talked. The dog kept getting meaner and bigger. I remembered that when the dog charged out from under the house, I was almost certain I'd seen foam on it's jowls.

Helen Maude's eyes shone with admiration. Doris' face took on an aura of awe. I'd never seen her look at me that way.

"Yeah, Ah felt his hot breath in mah face," I said. "His teeth looked an inch long an' he'd a bit me, if Ah hadn't jerked my head to the side."

I thought about saying, "If the dog had caught me by the throat an' Ah hadn't jerked my head out of the way, why Ah wouldn't be here now. Ah'd be in heaven with the angels. And evah'body down on earth would be cryin' 'cause Ah wadden theah any moah." My thoughts were so real that I got all choked up and really did feel like crying.

Daddy Floyd didn't interrupt but he rolled his eyes. By this time I was too enraptured with my bravery that I didn't care. I imagined what it would be like in school on Monday, and how all the kids in my class would be gathered around me, hangin' on every word. Maybe even the principal would hear about my brush with death and have me give a speech on my heroism to a school assembly. I imagined telling them how'd I fought off a giant mad dog with my bare hands and saved my whole family from rabies. As for the boys who were always trying to lord it over me, I figured they'd all be jealous 'cause such an exciting thing had happened to me instead of them.

The sun was coming up by the time we finished breakfast. "Ah yuh goin' lookin' foah the mad dog?" Doris asked. The respect still showed in her voice.

"Soon as Ah get some clothes on." I was still in my nightshirt.

I pulled on a pair of overalls and even put on shoes, just in case I came upon the wounded beast and had to kick him off me. "Ah'm goin," I announced with bravado. Helen Maude clapped. Doris grinned and slapped me on the shoulder. "Atta boy, Jimmie."

Grandmother made me look even braver. "Floyd, ah yuh sure he'll be awl right?"

Daddy Floyd nodded. Was his chin quivering from fear or amusement? I decided it didn't matter. Cradling the .22 rifle under my right arm, I strode down the hall and stepped from the front porch into the yard. The girls and Grandmother followed me. Daddy Floyd hung back.

I found the blood trail and remembered that big game hunters in Africa called that a spoor. I figured I'd better not call it that, for Doris might revert to her old form and tell everybody at school that I was just acting "big."

I followed the trail through the corn patch and came upon a little dog laying between two rows. I was shocked. Could this really be the animal I had shot? He was skin and bones and looked no bigger than a puppy. He didn't look like a wild dog at all. And he didn't froth about the mouth. I suddenly realized that this must have been somebody's pet that got lost, became hungry, and wandered into our back yard seeking food.

When I came closer the half-grown dog lifted his head in trust, showing no fear whatever. He looked at me through pain etched eyes. He struggled to get to his feet, and I saw the bloody, shattered left shoulder dangling toward the ground. Standing with head hanging and tongue lolling out of its mouth, the dog panted hoarsely. Painfully, he lifted his head to look straight into my eyes.

A thought hit me with a jolt: what if this had been my dog, Sport and he had wandered into some other farmer's yard and been shot?

I couldn't leave the helpless animal to die a slow, painful death in the corn field. I knew instinctively what I had to do.

I raised my rifle and sighted at a spot between the dog's eyes. Just before I squeezed off the shot, the wounded animal wagged his tail at me. I lowered the gun then turned my back on the dog and lifted the .22 again. I had put the dog in this condition, and I had no right to ask Daddy Floyd to finish him off. The merciful thing, the brave thing was to shoot the dog so he wouldn't linger in pain for days. Gritting my teeth in resolve, I turned quickly, aimed and pulled the trigger before those trusting eyes could look too long into mine. The dog's head slumped and his body dropped into the sand.

On the way back to the house I pondered the unfairness of a puppy having to die for simply trying to live. But trailing close behind that thought came the realization that chicken eggs were Grandmother's cash crop. And these were the desperate Depression years. There was no humane society in Newton County, Mississippi, to protect farmers from predators. They had to do that for themselves.

Daddy Floyd met me at the door of his shop where he had come to sharpen a plow for Uncle Ban. "Ah heard the shot," he said.

"Yeah," I grunted.

"Did yuh get pleasuah out of killing 'im?"

"Oh, no sir. Not a bit." I dabbed at my eyes. "It was jus' awful." I couldn't bring myself to say that our "wild" dog was just a half-grown puppy.

"Good! Ah'm glad yuh got no joy from finishing off a wounded animal. That was a hahd thing to do, Jimmie, but it was the right thing to do."

That helped — but only a little.

I stalled around to keep from encountering my aunts. Doris came running out anyway. "Did yuh kill the mad dog, Jimmie?"

"Yeah." The word congealed in my throat.

I brushed past her. Helen Maude came out of the kitchen where she had been helping Grandmother. "Did yuh finish the job?"

"Yeah." It still felt painful to answer.

Grandmother had overheard. "You'ah a brave boy, Jimmie," she said. "We'ah all proud of yuh."

I wanted to dispute her words. I wanted to tell her I had only killed a puppy.

I couldn't get the words out. "Grandmother," I said. "Ah'm goin' over to George Snowden's house an' see if he wants to go fishin'."

I didn't even tell George that I had shot a puppy.

Chapter 14

"The Great Snipe Hunt"

Having friends over to spend the night was a big deal for Mississippi farm youngsters in the 1930's. Being a year older than I, Doris got the privilege first.

"Jimmie Rogers, yuh keep out of owah way," she ordered. "Stay in youah room or go outside.

I kept out of their hair when they played with paper dolls or made cookies. When they moved into the parlor to play records on our stand-up Victrola, I sneaked a cookie and casually walked into their presence.

Doris handed me a icy look that said, "Awright, Jimmie Rogers, but if yuh do one liddle ole thang to mess up mah party, Ah'm gonna pull youah red haah out and throw yuh to the hawgs!"

I didn't give her any guff. Doris ran a tight ship when her friends were there. She couldn't afford to get a reputation in her circle for being nice to what she called "mah ugly red-headed nephew." Not wanting to incur her wrath, most of the time I stayed on my best behavior.

One Monday after school I heard a familiar big-boy voice.

"Hey, Jimmie!"

I turned to see Billy Joe Johnson. He had thick black hair and was two grades ahead and three years older than I. A big rough-and-tumble boy with three fun-loving brothers. What stunt Billy Joe couldn't think up, Edwin, Harley and Tom Johnson could.

"Wanna spend Friday night at owah house?" Billy Joe asked. "We'll have owahseves a pile of fun?"

I loved "spending the night" with other boys. A couple of weeks before Grandmother had let me have Ray McGee and two more friends over. She spread quilt pallets across the floor for us and we lay there listening to Daddy Floyd's ghost stories: "He's on the first step an' he's a comin' to getcha — he's on the second step an' he's a comin' to getcha…" Then when Daddy Floyd left, we made up our own and scared ourselves even more.

I heard Billy Joe's tantalizing voice again. "Yuh wanna come, Jimmie? If yuh don't, Ah can ask somebody else."

I really wanted to go. I didn't mention to Billy Joe that I'd have to check with my grandparents first. "Can Ah let yuh know tomorrow?" I asked.

He made a wry face. "Ah guess so."

Daddy Floyd didn't see any problem, but Grandmother did. "Those Johnson boys are oldah than yuh, Jimmie. Thea'ah growin' up to be rounders cause they don't get enough gentling from their mother."

"Aw, thea'ah awl right. Can Ah go? Please, Grandmothah. Please. Ah'll be hoam by suppah' time the next day."

Grandmother gave in. I later learned she was more right than even she knew. Amos Johnson was a big, rough construction man and the four boys were coming up as crude as their daddy. They could lie with a straight face and sound like God's blessed angels. They didn't mean to hurt anybody, but all too often they got out of control. Mrs. Johnson finally threw her hands up in the face of impossible odds and let her husband handle the boys.

Of course, Grandmother didn't know all this when she gave in to my plea for permission to spend the night at the Johnsons.

I told Billy Joe the next day that I could come. I shared my good news with other boys in my grade so they'd start giving me more respect.

To my astonishment, Ray McGee, remarked, "Wael, it looks lack them Johnson boys done foun' 'em anothah' fool."

"Whatcha mean?" I bristled at my classmate.

Ray looked me straight in the eye. "You'ah jus' plain stupid, Jimmie. Thea'ah plannin' to pull some kind of trick on yuh. Bet mah cat's eye shootah on it."

I knew he must be very serious if he was willing to risk his new marble shooter, a cat's eye at that. I'd been bragging about being singled out to be the guest of the Johnson boys; now I was beginning to feel more victim than guest.

"Whadayuh think they have in mind?" I inquired uneasily.

Ray shoved his hands deep down in his pockets and squinted his eyes tightly. This was his thoughtful mode and I could almost see smoke coming out of the top of his head. I didn't interrupt. Ray didn't like that.

"Wael, they won't really hurt yuh but theah'll prob'ly try to scah' yuh real bad."

Then his face lighted up. "Theah'll lackly take yuh snipe huntin'."

"Whut's a snipe? Ah heard Brothah and Nell talkin' 'bout snipe huntin' onct, but they wudden tell me what a snipe was."

Shaking his head, Ray looked at me in extreme disgust. "Jimmie Rogers, theah's no hope foah yuh, nevah wuz an' nevah will be. Ah don't think yuh even know what makes the grass grow. If yuh don't know theah's no such thing as a snipe then theah's no hope atall foah yuh. Yuh might jus' as well go on down to the State Insane Asylum at Meridian an' turn youah'sef in. Jus' tell 'um you'ah too much of a fool to be 'lowed to assoc'ate with noahmal folks, an' to jus' lock yuh up so's yuh can't hurt youah'sef or anybody else"

When Ray got wound up he could go on and on. He was like a broken alarm clock that started ringing high upon a high shelf and you had to wait until the spring wound down for it to stop. Finally, he calmed down and explained the snipe hunting trick and some other pretty low-down, dirty stunts the Johnson boys had pulled. I felt prepared but I figured it wouldn't hurt if I stayed very cautious and suspicious.

At the Johnsons that afternoon we shot marbles for awhile. We quit when Billy Joe and Harley got mad because all I'd play was "Dead Man." They wanted to play "Big Circle" but I knew better than to play their game. Their daddy had brought home some giant ball bearings from the garage where he kept his big construction equipment. One of those apple-sized bearings could clear almost every marble out of the big circle. After the marble game ended in a huff, we practiced shooting at tin cans with our slingshots until Mrs. Johnson called us in for supper.

It was almost like eating with a pack of wild dogs the way those boys grabbed and tore at the food. Mr. Johnson wasn't much better. Mrs. Johnson had played it safe and filled her plate before she called us all in to supper. Those boys may have broken her spirit but at least they hadn't killed her will to live. She even wrestled the mashed potatoes away from Tom once so I could get a helping. For a minute I thought he was going to win. After that I grabbed for food real quick when nobody was looking. I learned how to survive that night and I understood Mrs. Johnson better.

After supper we sat on the back porch steps watching the stars come out. After a while Tom said, "Boy, it sho' looks lack a good night fo' snipes."

My heart leaped, but remembering Ray's instructions, I pretended to be only mildly interested.

"Whut's a snipe?" I asked in pretended innocence.

All four boys, talking at once, told me in great detail how snipes were just about the best eating in the whole wide world. I did just what Ray told me to do. "Would y'all take me snipe huntin' sometime?"

Well, now. Those four boys debated back and forth until Billy finally told his brothers that I was one of his very best school friends and if they'd take me snipe hunting that night he'd personally vouch for me. Sure enough, to my total lack of surprise, his three brothers agreed, and they carefully explained how to catch the wily snipes. My job was to kneel in the big drainage ditch that ran through the woods to Chunky River, holding a croaker sack open to catch the snipes. A croaker sack is a burlap bag in the North. Southerners use it to catch frogs, thus the name "croaker sack."

"How will Ah know whut a snipe looks like?" I asked.

Billy Joe couldn't exactly describe one, but "you'll know a snipe when yuh see it," he assured me. "Now me an' mah brothahs ah gonna' run up the ditch a liddle ways an' shoo the snipes down tow'd yuh. Them snipes ah so dumb," he said, "they'll jus' run right into youah croaker sack."

I played the scene like a born actor, pretending to be grateful for the privilege of holding the sack. They clamped their lips real tight so as not to laugh when I asked if we could sell all the snipes we got that we couldn't eat. They didn't speak but just nodded their heads vigorously, signifying "yes."

We crept down through the deep woods and they left me in the ditch with my croaker sack after explaining they'd have to take the lanterns with them. Snipes, Tom said, wouldn't go near a kerosene light because of the smell. "Ah know a lot of fokes who think they'ah good snipe huntahs but they can't catch any 'cause they don't take their lantuhns a long ways away. Now, Jimmie you've gotta promise us you won't tell anybody what we catch so's theah'll be plenty of snipes foah us the nex' time."

I was biting the inside of my lip—hard—while he spoke and I answered with the quick pledge, "Ah won't."

If I'd said one word more I'd have busted out laughing. Watching and listening very carefully as the lanterns faded through the woods, I clearly heard their titters and hoarse whispers.

"He don't s'pect nuthin," I heard Tom say.

"Yeah, he' so dumb he wudden undahstand even if we wuz to tell 'im," Billy Jo chirped.

I smiled to myself in delightful anticipation. I'd show 'em who was dumb.

I let them get about a hundred yards away before taking out my pocket knife. I cut big slices in the croaker sack to give the appearance of being clawed by a wildcat. Then I gouged up the dirt all around the spot where I was standing to make it look like a terrible fight had taken place. If I'd had my thinking cap on, I would have brought a bottle of ketchup to "bloody" the ground. Still I figured they'd think a wildcat had killed me and carried me off.

With the slaughter scene prepared I gave two loud screams, and took off toward the house like a scalded dog, not stopping until I stepped in the side yard. I crept up close to the window of the parents' bedroom and heard snores. Good fortune was smiling on me, for the dogs were with the four Johnson boys down in the ditch. I lifted the window to the boys' room, climbed inside, and piled down on the pallet which Mrs. Johnson had spread for me on the floor. There I lay awaiting the return of the real fools. There I fell fast asleep.

Meanwhile, the Johnson boys, after hiding and waiting for a long time in the woods, snuffed out their lanterns and sneaked back to the spot where they had left me holding the croaker sack. On signal, they all jumped out screaming like banshees hoping to scare the bejiggers out of me—but, of course, I was gone. They lit their lanterns and saw my sack ripped to shreds and the terrible gouges in the dirt. Remembering the screams, they immediately jumped to my hoped-for, horrible conclusion.

After an earnest consultation among themselves, they decided their lives wouldn't be worth a plugged nickel if they went home to their daddy without me, so they began a desperate search. After a couple of hours, they had another conference and decided "Old" Mexico was too far to run, so they fearfully trudged home and roused their dad to tell him they had lost me in the woods.

I became aware that all was not well when I was awakened out of a deep sleep by the Johnson boys hollering and screaming in the back yard. Slipping out on the darkened back porch, I beheld a bizarre sight. Mr. Johnson was whirling about in his long, flannel nightshirt holding a lantern in one hand and swinging a buggy whip with the other at the legs of four dancing boys.

"Whut do yuh mean, yuh lost Jimmie? You don't jus' lose a boy out theah amongs the wildcats an' God only knows what else. Now yuh jus' bettah tell me the truth or ah'm gonna whale the livin' tar out of all of yuh. How do yuh think ah'm gonna 'splain to Mistah James what happened to his gran'boy? He set lots'a stock by that boy." I noticed he used the past tense. He must have thought I was lying dead somewhere.

All the while he was yelling he kept swinging that "hoss stinger" and striping the legs of his boys. Up till then I didn't know how well the Johnson boys could dance. It was a classic case of ambivalence. They wanted to skedaddle but they were more scared of what would happen if they ran than of what would happen if they stayed.

The boys were hopping up and down hollering and yelling at the top of their lungs.

"Wait a minnit, Papa!"

"Ow, that hurts!"

"Jus' lissen now, Papa!," Tom pleaded. "We kin fin' 'im! Papa jus' put that whup down an' we'll go look some moah foah Jimmie! Ah believe Ah knows wheah he is, now that Ah think about it!"

Rubbing my eyes, I advanced farther out on the back porch and stepped into the lantern light. Tom saw me first. His eyes popped wide open as if he saw a ghost. He stabbed his finger at me and screamed, "Theah he is, Papa!"

All eyes turned toward me as the boys stared in open-mouthed disbelief. They had really thought a wildcat had carried me off. And Mr. Johnson? His mouth creased into an even tighter line as he turned and began flailing all about with renewed vigor.

"Ah knowed it. Ah knowed it. Yuh boys knowed all along he wuz in yoah room. You'ah jus tryin' to drive me crazy an' nex' time yuh try, you'ah gonna have wus' than striped laigs."

Finally, Mr. Johnson's arm got tired and he went back to bed, still fussing under his breath. My "friends" slipped back into the bedroom only to find me missing.

Billy Joe, followed by Harley, crept out into the darkened hall. "Jimmie, oh, Jimmie. Yuh out heah?"

I had moved my pallet to a spot just outside Mr. and Mrs. Johnson's bedroom door.

Billy Joe found me. "Ah, Jimmie, there yuh ah. Come on back in owah room with us. It's a lot coolah theah."

"Yeh, come on, Jimmie," Harley begged. "We ain't mad."

I turned over and moaned, pretending to be in pain.

That awoke their mother who hollered at their father.

"Amos, whut's that noise outside owah door? Sounds lack a bunch of dawgs."

Mr. Johnson's feet hit the floor. His sons went slithering back into their room. Holding on to my pallet, I crawled quietly down to the other end of the hall.

The next morning silence roared around the breakfast table and the glares in my direction were so powerful I could have walked on them. When the school bus came to a stop in front of the Johnson's house I stayed by the front door thanking Mrs. Johnson until her boys got on the bus. Then just as the bus was ready to pull away I rushed out, dashed up the steps and stood in front beside the driver even though there were several empty seats.

Daddy Floyd's only grandson was no fool after all. When the bus reached school I jumped off first and quickly ran over to George Snowden. The Johnson boys knew that I was George's best friend and they had better sense than to trifle with him.

After a few days the Johnson boys began to talk to me again, but they didn't invite me to do anything else with them for over two years.

When I told Ray McGee all the bloody details, he almost split a gut laughing. "Jimmie," he said, "Ah've gotta give it to yuh, boy. Yuh ain't as dumb as Ah thought yuh was."

Chapter 15

"The Artesian Well"

Delightful memories of the great snipe hunt soon took second place to talk of an artesian well in the pasture. Daddy Floyd had to endure all of mine and Doris' questions:

"What's wrong with the well we've got?"

"It's only a dug well. The watah just seeps into it below ground."

"What's so special 'bout an artesian well?"

"The watah is trapped under a ceiling of rock an' clay. When yuh drill way down an' break that barrier, the pressuh is released an' the watah shoots up. It'll be lack havin' a big watah fountain in owah paschah," Daddy Floyd said.

"Who's gonna drill it?"

"We've got a big crew comin'. They'll break through the rock an' clay and release the watah."

"How they gonna know wheah to drill?"

"A water witcher is comin' with them. He'll tell them wheah."

Daddy Floyd finally got tired of answering our questions. "When they come yuh can watch," he promised. "Long as it isn't a school day. As long as yuh don't get in the way."

Right in the middle of all the waiting, Mother came for a surprise two-day visit. Helen Maude asked her right out if she had a boy friend. The way Mother blushed made us suspicious: "Of co'se I've got a boy friend. Moah than one. But I haven't decided yet. When I do get married, Jimmie will be comin' to live with me."

The way she smiled showed that I was still the most important person in her life. Not wanting to hurt Mother's feelings, I didn't say what I was thinking: "Ah hope yuh won't get married 'fo the men come to dig the artesian well."

Mother stayed until Friday afternoon of that week when she bade us another tearful goodbye at the Meridian station. When we got back to the farm, Daddy Floyd casually announced, "The drillers an' the watah witcher will be heah in the mawnin', Yuh chirrun get a good night's sleep. Ah'll wake yuh early so yuh won't miss a thing."

I drifted off to dreamland. The next sound I heard was Daddy Floyd: "Wake up, Jimmie, it's 'bout time foah the men to come an' drill the artesian well."

At first I thought Daddy Floyd was part of my dream but then the sweet smell of bacon frying in the kitchen teased my nostrils. My eyes popped open and I bounced out of bed.

"Wheah ah they? Ah they heah?" I gasped.

For one panicky moment I feared Daddy Floyd had let the well diggers start without me. But as fast as the thought came, it went.

Daddy Floyd wouldn't let that happen. He wouldn't open the pasture gate until I got there. He'd promised. And grandfathers didn't break promises to ten-year-old grandsons.

"Get youah clothes on, son, an' get youah breakfas' down. Ah reckon they'ah crossin' Okahatta Creek down in the swamp 'bout now."

Quickly I stepped into my overalls and pulled them up as I pitched my night shirt over my head. It sailed in the air and came down on the floor.

"Gittin' closah," I mused to myself. "Neahbout hit mah dresser this time."

The cool March morning called for a flour sack shirt and shoes and socks. Tying my high topped, mail order shoes, I wondered if the weather would warm up enough to remove them later. I hoped so.

I raced into the kitchen and poured cane syrup over two of Grandmother's big, fluffy biscuits. Halfway through gobbling down the biscuits and syrup the wind shifted and I clearly heard a deep rumble from the swamp.

"Grandmothah, get me a couple of bacon biscuits to take with me," I requested.

"Now, take youah time, Jimmie. The crew won't be heah foah a spell, so yuh can jus' calm down."

"Ah can't wait. Ah gotta go!"

Rushing out of the kitchen, I ran out to the road by the shop expecting to see the truck start up the clay hill by the piney woods at the edge of the swamp.

As I took up my position by Daddy Floyd's shop, Doris came ambling out on the porch to wash her face and brush her hair. Every morning she did that.

Grandmother didn't tell her to do it, she just did. It seemed like a waste of time to me.

"Doris, yuh bettah hurry, they'ah coming."

She glared at me in eleven-year-old majesty. "Shut up, fool!"

Doris never was in a very good mood when she first woke up. I hoped she'd improve as the day moved on. Cecil and Vernell were still working away from home. Helen Maude had spent the night at a girl friend's house. That left me and Doris to see the big event.

Drying her face, Doris called to Grandmother. "Mothah, Ah feel like a big slow breakfas'."

I almost laughed out loud. She was going to miss the arrival of the well-digging outfit for sure, and I almost couldn't stand it because I was so glad. After a few minutes Grandmother came out with my bacon biscuits wrapped up in a couple of pages of yesterday's **Meridian Star**.

"They'ah almost heah," I told her hopefully.

"Don't yuh want to wait in the house, Jimmie. It's pretty cool heah in the yard."

"No maam, Ah'm awright. It's not too cold," I said with a shiver.

After several minutes Daddy Floyd came in from feeding the animals in the barn. "Jimmie, why in the world ah yuh out heah in the cold. Didn't Doris tell yuh it would take the men 'bout an owah to pump the watah truck full from the creek? Ah told her when she first got up to be sure an' tell yuh."

I dashed to the house to confront Doris. "Yuh knew—yuh knew all along, but yuh jus' had to let me stay out heah an' freeze."

My fussy, smart-tongued auntie perched on a chair at the kitchen table, lazily spreading watermelon rind preserves on her biscuit with a knife. She took a big bite, smacked her lips, and finally acknowledged my presence.

"No, Ah didden do that, Jimmie. Ah jus' watched while yuh froze all by youah'sef."

"Grandmothah, did yuh heah that? Did yuh heah what she did to me?" I wailed. "Yuh gotta do somthin' 'bout that girl. It's a dangah to be in the same room with her—the same farm—no, the same world."

Doris drew her head up and tilted it back in the way that made me so mad and sniffed, "You'ah jus' sayin' that 'cause you'ah so stupid."

"Grandmothah! Did yuh heah that? That's the kind of talk Ah hafta put up with all the time."

Grandmother had been stirring something on the stove. Now she turned slowly and gazed frostily, first at Doris, then at me.

"When Ah woke up this morning Ah said to mahsef that Ah would take unkindly to anybody who messed up mah day. Do yuh two know anybody who might do that?"

As she spoke in measured tones, she shook her big wooden spoon at us, accenting each syllable. Doris and I decided on the spot that we'd better be elsewhere. Lips sealed, we scooted out of the house to wait for the well-diggers by the road.

After what seemed like hours, we heard the big engines roar to life down in the swamp and move in our direction. We looked across the cotton fields and after several minutes saw the top of a truck coming into view on the hill that rose above the swamp. As it progressed along the road we noticed it was leading a tank truck which pulled a four wheel, rubber-tired wagon loaded with pipe. The huge lead truck was an old chain-driven Mack and it looked like it was hauling a small oil derrick on its side.

I danced in excitement as the big Mack clanked and rattled on its solid rubber tires along the road to the house. Before the procession reached us, the excitement overcame me, and I had to race for the outhouse, with Doris screeching, "Whatsa mattah?" When I returned, the Mack and its entourage had ground to a stop by the front yard

Grandmother and Daddy Floyd stood waiting with Doris. Grandmother held a bucket and dipper. The driver jumped down from the Mack truck, tipped his hat to Grandmother and shook Daddy Floyd's hand. Two men stepped out of the second truck and two teenage boys slid down from their perches on top of the chained-down pipe.

"D'yall want a cold drink of watah from owah liddle dug well heah at the house?" Grandmother asked.

She held the bucket while each of the men and boys drank their fill and complimented Grandmother on how good her well water tasted.

After awhile the courtesies were completed and the men started up the trucks while Daddy Floyd struck out for the pasture gate to open it for the drillers and their equipment. He trotted through the gate and led the way down the lane, driving old Jude, the mule, pulling the slip. The slip was like a giant scoop shovel three feet wide with two huge handles that were flipped over to dump the load. Daddy Floyd held the reins and stood balanced on the back of the slip to keep it from digging in as Jude plodded ahead.

When the tank truck stopped at the farm gate, one of the teenage boys on top of the load of pipe asked if I wanted to ride with them up into the pasture where the new well was to be drilled.

Boy, howdy! Did I!

Acting as if it was nothing, I said only, "Well, Ah reckon so."

The boys reached down and pulled me up. I felt like I was sitting on a big, high throne. Doris didn't wait to be invited. She just jumped up and caught her foot in the bottom row of pipe. Using the pipe ends like a ladder, she climbed to the top, tossed me a superior smirk, and sat like a queen on her throne.

"They heped me up," I said, trying to sound superior.

"Ah'm big enough Ah didden need any help," was her acid response.

The procession rolled along until the lane broadened into the pasture and then they stopped. A big mustached man, wearing a straw hat and sitting next to the tank truck driver, stepped out and walked over to a water oak tree. Cutting off a small limb with equal forks he trimmed away all the offshoots and leaves, leaving a Y-shaped branch.

"That's the watah witcher," Doris whispered in awe.

I couldn't resist the temptation to say it: "Takes a witch to know one."

Doris stuck out her tongue and would have said something nasty had the water witcher not spoken.

"Ah lak' to use a limbah willow limb t'do this but this'en'll do."

Grasping the two forks of the branch at the ends, he held his hands in front of his chest so the stem was pointing directly ahead.

As he walked back and forth across the pasture the point kept dipping down and then up. At one point he called out, "Theah's sumthin' heah foah sure 'nuf, but Ah ain't foun' the stream yet."

He kept muttering to himself as he walked, spitting out an occasional stream of tobacco juice. Each time he did this, I looked over at Grandmother and saw her upper lip curl in disgust. She purely hated tobacco chewing and snuff dipping.

Narrowing his search, the water witcher walked a zig-zag line toward the lowest part of the pasture. All of a sudden, it seemed like a giant unseen hand grabbed the end of his stick and jerked it all the way down to the ground, pulling him down to his knees.

"Whoooeee! Heah's youah watah an' a whole lots of it! Theah's a rivah down theah below!" he shouted.

I looked at Grandmother. She had never believed in water witching but even she now joined in our excitement.

Daddy Floyd turned his slip right side up and in short order old Jude scooped out a round depression about fifteen feet in diameter and two feet deep. As the Mack truck backed up and raised the derrick in the upright position the tank truck driver began dumping some of his creek water in the hole the mule had scooped out. The men quickly hooked onto the first length of pipe and attached a cutter to the bottom end.

Doris and I looked on with wonder.

The driller now addressed Daddy Floyd. "Ah'm puttin' on a cheap sand cuttah, Mr. James. If we don't hit rock Ah can leave it down theah but if Ah hafta put on a rock cuttah Ah'll hafta draw all the pipe back out to git mah cuttah back."

Daddy Floyd nodded.

The men attached a water flushing fitting to the top of the pipe and connected a hose to it. Then they hooked up the other end of the hose to a small gasoline powered pump. "Tha's to wash out the dirt as we drill it," the driller explained.

The drilling began and I never heard such a racket in all my life. The un-muffled big engine on the Mack truck roared and the small water pump engine screamed in a high pitched whine. It was so loud they had to move back a hundred feet or more just to talk to each other. The drill pipe bit into the dirt and bored through to sand forty feet down.

"Tha's a good sign, Mr. James. Most times, sand means lots of watah," shouted the driller over the din.

The drilling went fast. The water brought from the creek spouted out of the upper end of the pipe with sand as the lower end bit deeper into the ground. The two teenage boys worked frantically to shovel out the sand in the pit scooped out by Daddy Floyd as it fell into the pit filled with the warm creek water.

After about two hours of hard drilling the water witcher held up his hand. He had taken off his shoes, and now he walked back and forth barefooted along the rim of the hole. He seemed to be listening—no, feeling with his bare feet. We all watched him, scarcely breathing, not knowing what to expect. He stopped walking and began to rock from heel to heel lifting each foot only an inch or so off the ground. Slowly a smile flickered across his face. Then a broad grin.

"Folks, yoah drill pipe is jus' ten feet from cool, sweet watah."

The driller looked up and saw he had more than ten feet of pipe in the air and he told his men to remove the flushing fitting from the pipe and shut down the pump. As the drilling started again, the witcher called out over the roar of the big engine, "Folks, keep youah eyes on the end of the pipe."

When the top of the pipe dropped to about four feet above the ground, we heard a gentle swoosh and water came gushing out of the pipe. It was cloudy at first but in no more than two minutes it was pure and clean as could be. The driller eased the end of the pipe down to two feet above the surface and disconnected the drilling rig from it.

He called over to the teenage boys. "D'yuh boys wanna cool off?"

They looked at each other and in one voice answered, "Sho' do!"

The driller tossed an elbow fitting to the nearest boy. "Screw this on the end of the pipe."

Then he tapped Daddy Floyd on the arm with his fingers and I overheard him say, "Watch this, Mr. James, them boys is new to this work."

The boys rushed in with the fitting and tried to screw it onto the end of the pipe. Well, water gushed everywhere! And was it cold! But the two boys were determined and in spite of the water pressure and the cold, cold water squirting all over them they screwed on the fitting and tightened it firmly with a big Stilson pipe wrench.

The boys stumbled out of the knee-deep, bone-chilling water coming from deep underground. They danced around slapping themselves to warm up. Everybody laughed, watching them. Later the men screwed on a horizontal piece of pipe to keep the gushing water from eroding away the dirt around the vertical pipe. Their last act was to move a huge wooden water trough under the flow of water. The flow was so great the trough filled in seconds.

The driller grinned at Daddy Floyd. "Mister James, theah's en'uff water down theah to slake the thirst of evah cow in Newton County."

Daddy Floyd spoke in appreciation. "Yuh fellahs did a good job."

"Yeah, mah crew knows whut to do. But first the witcher's gotta find the watah."

187

The witcher nodded his agreement and to Grandmother's disgust spat a long stream of brown tobacco juice into the trough.

"Aw'right, let's wrap it up," the driller commanded.

The men lowered the drilling rig to the horizontal position behind the truck while the boys chained down the remaining pipe. In no time at all they were rumbling up the lane to the house.

Grandmother had asked Aunt Lizzie to fix a big dinner for the crew and they smelled the food as they closed the lane gate. By the time they got cleaned up at the wash stand on the back porch they were famished. Doris and I ate with the boys at the kitchen table while the grown-ups ate in the dining room. Aunt Lizzie bustled around with huge bowls of mashed potatoes, black eyed peas, turnip greens and platters piled high with fried chicken.

Doris had been batting her eyes at the teenage boys. Now she turned to me and said, "Jimmie, do yuh want some moah of this fried chicken?"

I felt the hair rise on the back of my neck and I looked suspiciously at her, expecting some sort of trick, but she was actually smiling at me!

I reckoned I never would understand that girl.

Chapter 16

"Mean Simon Bolivar"

Mistah Floyd?" The voice spoke low and cautious.

"Mistuh Floyd?"

I pried open my eyes, not certain I'd really heard anything. Sport had barked earlier, but how long before I wasn't sure.

The voice came again.

"Mistuh Floyd?"

This time the male whisper came a bit louder. I sensed a tone of anxiety, which I couldn't quite place. And I heard other muffled sounds which I couldn't make out coming from the back yard near the back porch steps. Daddy Floyd and Grandmother's bedroom was on the other side of the house and I feared he couldn't hear the voice. The boys' bedroom where I slept opened to the back porch with only a screen door and a few feet separating me from the anxious whisperer.

"Mistuh Floyd!" The voice was louder still and now I recognized it. I'd heard Arsene's voice in the cotton field last fall. Arsene singing with his wife,

Lena; her sister, Callie, and Callie's husband, Wilmer. Two of Daddy Floyd's black sharecropping couples harmonizing,

> Gonna jump down, turn around,
> *Pick a bale o' cotton;*
> *Gonna jump down, turn around,*
> *Pick a bale o' cotton,*
> *Pick a bale a day.*
> *Oh, Lawdy, pick a bale o' cotton,*
> *Oh Lawdy, pick a bale a day.*

I was about to call across the hall to Daddy Floyd when I heard his sleepy voice. "Jus' a minute." Arising, I slipped quietly over to the screen door, opening to the backyard, to see the whisperer. In the bright moonlight, I could clearly see Arsene and Wilmer.

Back in the shadows of the chinaberry tree nearest my room I could barely see three more figures. At that moment Daddy Floyd came onto the back porch from the kitchen through the corner of the dining room. He wore a pair of trousers under his night shirt and carried the glass coal oil lamp from his bedroom nightstand.

"That yuh, Arsene?"

"Yassah, Mistuh Floyd, an' Wilmah, an' owah wimmin fokes."

Another voice which I recognized as Arsene's wife, Lena, spoke.

"Willie, liddle brothah t'me an' Callie is heah too, Mistuh Floyd."

With that she led a thin, young boy of about eighteen out of the shadows — and what a frightful sight he was. He looked more dead than alive. Caked-on blood and dirt covered his face and spattered his ragged overalls and shirt. Walnut-sized knots bulged from the left side of his head and his left eye was completely swollen shut. His left ear, torn at the top where it attached to his head, hung down noticeably. His arms were crossed tightly across his body, clutching his ribs as though to constrain his heaving chest. His breath came in great gasping sobs and he shook all over with uncontrollable tremors. Only a hair breath away from a state of physical shock, he had obviously been terrorized. I felt acid rising in the pit of my stomach.

Again, Lena spoke. And now she began to cry.

"Oh, Mistuh Floyd, luk whut Mistuh Bolivar dun t'mah liddle brothah, Willie."

Daddy Floyd saw. His face froze. He knew the white farmer for which Willie had been working for pittance wages. Through clenched teeth, he said, "Did Simon Bolivar do this to yuh, Willie?"

Poor Willie couldn't speak, but painfully and slowly he nodded his head three or four times.

Grandmother, now awake, had caught sight of Willie. "Bring that poah boy in heah so Ah can tend tuh 'im."

Lena and Arsene helped Willie up the back porch steps, and guided him through the kitchen door. Grandmother told them to seat Willie on the end of the bench at the kitchen table. I couldn't see them any longer from my position by the back porch, so I ran around through the hall to the dining room door leading into the kitchen.

"What happened?" Doris whispered in my ear. She had heard the voices from the girls' bedroom in the front of the house and was as curious as I.

"Ah dunno. Ah think he got whupped real bad by somebody."

Grandmother had a way of taking charge of situations and she did so now. Helen Maude stood at the girls' bedroom door, between Daddy Floyd's bedroom and the kitchen. Grandmother started what Daddy Floyd called her "go-get-me's" by turning to Helen Maude and saying, "Go get me a quilt from the quilt closet. This boy's cold as ice." Grandmother called to the visitors: "Willmah, go get me a foot tub from the back porch. Callie, fill it with watah from the hot watah reservoir on the stove. Helen Maude, go get me mah medicine kit."

In no time at all Willie was seated with a quilt around his trembling body with both feet in the foot tub of hot water. Lena rubbed his arms gently and Grandmother washed dried blood and dirt off his face and applied medication to his wounds. Now and then she spoke quietly to Willie, saying things like, "You'ah safe now; don't be scahed." And, "this is goin' to hurt some but Ah can't hep it."

Finally, Willie was cleaned up, with liniment on the swellings and mercurochrome on the small cuts and scratches. Grandmother applied salve to the larger open cuts to keep the bandages from sticking. The bandage pads were made from a torn-up old pillow case and held on by adhesive.

Willie's ear was the most troublesome. Grandmother looked at it and said to Lena, "Ah could sew it back up, but in the shape he's in Ah don't think he could take the pain. Maybe we oughta take him to see Doctuh Gilmore."

At that Lena quickly exclaimed, "Oh, no ma'am, Miz Jennie! Iffen he goes tuh the doctah, Mistuh Bolivar is gon' fin' out wheah he's stayin'."

Grandmother heaved a big sigh. "All right, let's jus' tape it an' hope the wound closes up."

She tore pieces of adhesive tape about three inches long from the roll and cut notches in the middle from both sides, leaving only about a third of the tape left. Taping the tear closed, she then taped his ear flat against his head. It had been several hours since the ear had been torn and the numbness had worn off, but Willie never flinched as Grandmother worked to repair the ear.

Daddy Floyd walked to the garage, backed the car out and drove into the back yard. It was only about a hundred and fifty yards to the first sharecrop house, but Willie couldn't have walked more than fifty feet in his condition. Arsene and Wilmer helped him into the car and all but Wilmer got in. He stood on the running board while Daddy Floyd drove them home.

After they left, Helen Maude, Doris and I boldly moved into the kitchen to find out more details about Willie's beating. "Tonight wadden the time to question that poah boy," Grandmother told us. "Now yuh chirren get on back to bed an' get some sleep."

The next day was Saturday and Willie slept all day long. About supper time he awakened and Lena quickly prepared some gruel and warmed a bowl of thin soup for him. He ate as much as he could and slept all Saturday night. Arsene stayed at home with him Sunday while the rest of the group went to church. Willie awakened and talked a little to Arsene while he ate. With each bite he regained a little more strength.

While staying with him Sunday, Arsene learned the whole story, then walked up to our house in the afternoon to tell Daddy Floyd. I hung close to catch as much as I could.

Willie had been "running around" cotton for Simon Bolivar, when the episode occurred. Running around cotton is the most precise plowing there is on a farm. The plow is only a small, six-inch point share attached to a sharp floating wing that extends about ten inches on each side of the point. The object is not to allow the wing to dig in but to draw back slightly on the plow handles against the pull of the mule. This allows the plow wings to float like a pendulum about an inch below the surface of the ground to slice grass and weed roots. On the right side a vertical guard about ten inches wide extends down to the ground to prevent dirt from being thrown against the base of the cotton plants.

Willie's problem was a young fidgety mule. He couldn't do this meticulous plowing, requiring both hands on the plow handles, while still having to fight the mule. The nervous mule had caused Willie to plow into the cotton rows three times that day, each time cutting down about four plants. The last time it had happened, Simon Bolivar had become enraged and attacked Willie like a mad man. He beat Willie unmercifully with a three-foot long singletree — a far more deadly weapon than a baseball bat because of its metal projections. Made of wood, a singletree has metal attach points around the middle and both ends to connect the plow beam with the harness.

Arsene told Daddy Floyd in horror, "Mistuh Bolivar, he beat Willie tuh the ground with that singletree. He said, 'Ah'm goin' tuh th' house tuh git mah gun an' Ah'm gonna kill yuh, boy.' We's the only kin Willie's got in this county, Mistuh Floyd, an' he come tuh us."

Willie, Arsene said, had started running up the road, about six in the evening, toward Daddy Floyd's farm — a distance of almost twelve miles. When he saw cars coming he hid in the ditches, fearful that Simon Bolivar was looking for him. His terror increased until he was on the verge of shock when he finally arrived at his sisters'.

Daddy Floyd's eyes turned steel-grey. I'd never seen him so enraged and it frightened me. Struggling to control his speech, he spoke in an angry whisper. "We've gotta protect Willie from Simon Bolivar."

Daddy Floyd was building a new cotton gin for a businessman in Hickory and Arsene and Wilmer were working with him for day wages. I'd been going along to help as much as I could. "Willie'd bettah go to town with us foah the nex' few days," Daddy Floyd told Arsene. "Simon Bolivar won't daah lay a hand on Willie if Ah'm around."

So Willie went with us to work Monday through Saturday. Saturday night, Grandmother removed the bandages except for the tape over his left arm. He went to church the next day with Arsene, Wilmer and his sisters and even smiled a little.

On the following Monday Willie again went to town with us. Daddy Floyd began to let Willie do some light work, like fetch nails and get tools. He wouldn't let Willie help carry the heavy timbers, though.

Dinner time came. "Willie," Daddy Floyd asked, "do yuh feel strong enough to go up to Simpson's stoah an' get us some Co'Cola's."

Eager to please, Willie answered, "Oh, yassuh, Mistuh James."

The Simpson family owned a service station with a small grocery store attached, a forerunner to the modern mini-mart. Willie walked the two blocks there in bright sunshine and went inside the dimly lit store. After waiting a few seconds for his eyes to adjust he gathered up what Daddy Floyd wanted and dropped the money on the counter. The door squeaked and he turned to look. Simon Bolivar was entering!

There was no back door so Willie rushed past his assailant whose eyes were still adjusting to the dark room. He was out the door before Simon Bolivar realized who had run by him. Bolivar ran and jumped into his pickup truck to chase Willie, catching up just as the young black reached Daddy Floyd who was standing beside a lumber pile.

Willie fell to his knees and locked his arms around Daddy Floyd's legs in desperate fear. "Oh,

Mistuh Floyd, don't let 'im kill me!" he shrieked in fright.

Arsene and I were just as petrified with fear as Willie when Simon Bolivar jumped out of his truck, carrying the biggest revolver in his hand I had ever seen.

"Ah want mah nigra!" he bellowed. "An' I aim to have 'im or Ah aim to kill 'im!"

I moved close to Arsene, paralyzed with fear.

Willie scooted on his knees around behind Daddy Floyd, without releasing his grip on his legs. Daddy Floyd held up his left hand, palm out, to Simon Bolivar. Reaching behind himself with his right hand, my grandfather pulled Willie to his feet without ever taking his eyes off Simon Bolivar. Willie stood trembling close behind Daddy Floyd trying to look even smaller than he was.

With eyes cold and brittle, Daddy Floyd said in a measured hard whisper. "This young man dudden b'long to yuh, Simon Bolivar. He don't belong to anybody. He's with me by his own free choice."

Saying that, he turned his head slightly, still watching the glowering brute, and asked. "D'ya want to go with 'im, Willie?"

Willie answered in a trembling whisper. "Oh, no suh, Mistuh James. Ah wont's tuh stay wif yuh."

Turning his full face to Simon Bolivar, Daddy Floyd said in a hoarse, frozen voice, "You ah in great dangah heah, Simon Bolivah. If yuh ah not gone from heah by the time Ah count to three, Ah'm goin' to take that gun away from yuh an' hurt yuh with it real bad."

"One!" Daddy Floyd pronounced.

Simon Bolivar dropped his eyes, stuck the gun in his belt and without a word spun on his heels, got in his truck and drove away.

I don't think I breathed during the whole exchange and now I let my breath out with a giant "whoosh."

Willie, pushed back emotionally to where he was a week before, crouched down behind the lumber pile and sobbed. I looked at him and anger built up inside of me. *"Nobody should be made to feah foah his life like that,"* I thought. *"It's not right."*

Daddy Floyd knew that Simon Bolivar wouldn't be back that day but to reassure Willie, he asked me to keep a close lookout for Willie's oppressor.

Later that afternoon, on the way out of town, Daddy Floyd dropped by the town marshall's office and spoke with him for a few minutes. "You fellahs stay outside an' keep watch," he told me and the young black men.

When Daddy Floyd emerged, I saw the butt of a revolver sticking out of the right side pocket of his carpenter coveralls. We didn't talk much on the way back to the farm.

I'd like to be writing fiction now so I could end the story the way I would've preferred it to end. But life is often different and stranger than fiction.

I was with Daddy Floyd the next morning when he stopped his car at the sharecrop house to pick up his workers. Willie wasn't with them. His sister, Lena, stood alone on the front porch, leaning against the door frame. She watched as Arsene and Wilmer got in the car. Her eyes smoldered in bitterness.

Daddy Floyd stepped out of the car and walked up on the porch. "Is Willie gone, Lena?"

"Yassuh. He gone, Mistuh James," she answered, using the formal address.

"Did somebody come, Lena?" asked Daddy Floyd softly.

"Ah'm not s'posed tuh say, Mistuh James."

"Were they weahin' white, Lena, an' drivin' a pickup truck?" persisted Daddy Floyd.

Lena nodded as her head dropped to her chest and tears, more bitter for the helplessness she felt, rolled from her eyes and down her cheeks.

I heard Daddy Floyd explode under his breath his worst curse word, "Thunderation!" Then he said, "Did they force him, Lena?"

"No suh, Mistuh James, they left in the truck, an' Willie, he jus' walk't back to Mistuh Bolivar by hisself."

Daddy Floyd looked intently at her for a long moment, then reached under her chin with his finger and tenderly lifted her tear-streaked face to look into her eyes. He said softly, "Lena, yuh DO know Ah'd have protected 'im, don't yuh?"

"Oh, yassuh, Mistuh Floyd," said Lena, reverting back to the personal address. "Ah truly do, but po' Willie wuz so scairt."

Daddy Floyd beckoned to me, Arsene and Wilmer. "Let's go to work." Once we were in the car, he turned and looked at Arsene and Wilmer in the back seat. "Theah's no way Ah can hep Willie if he stays with that man who beat 'im. If he comes back heah, Ah can help 'im."

"Yassuh, Mr. Floyd, we knows that, but Willie, he won't come," Arsene spoke in a dull flat voice.

Arsene, Wilmer and their wives moved up near Tupelo, Mississippi at the end of the harvest season. They didn't even winter at our farm, which they were entitled to do according to their sharecrop contract. We never heard any more of them or Willie.

Chapter 17

"Black Breed"

George Snowden, Otho Harris, Goober Brown and I sat in the shade of the bandstand in the Hickory town square. I was spinning a yarn about Uncle Semmy when George got everybody's attention.

"Tha's him! Tha's Black Breed!" George pointed to an enormous black man clomping past Chapman's Drugstore.

"Lookit the people skitterin' out of his way," Otho whispered. "Even white fokes step aroun' Black Breed."

Our eyes followed the most feared man in Newton County as he strode along the sidewalk. The Hickory town marshall stood six foot two, but Black Breed was taller, plus having a barrel-sized chest and stovepipe arms.

"He's gettin' in that ole Buick he made into a stake truck," George noted. "Ah wish he'd drive off an' nevah come back heah."

"Wheah yuh reckon he's goin'?" Otho pressed.

George shrugged. "Who caahs, so long as he stays away from Hickory."

"What's his name? Wheah'd yuh reckon he come from?" I asked George.

"All Ah've evah heard 'im called is 'Black Breed.' He jus' showed up in Hickory a couple of years ago. Moved into the nigra part of town. Kicked in the door of the biggest moonshiner down theah. Pa says he grabbed the man right in front of his wife and chirrun an' slammed him face down on the floor. Twisted both arms behind his back til they broke. Told the shiner's family if they caused him any trouble, he'd kill 'um all, cut 'um up and feed 'um to his hogs. Man's wife was scaahed to death an' wudden open her mouth to the sheriff.

"Black Breed," George continued, "got awl the shine business by scaahin' the bejeebies out of evah'body else makin' it."

Goober broke in. "Lookit, he's tuhnin' the corner. Ah hope he don't come back this way. Ah don't want him even lookin' at me."

Daddy Floyd and Grandmother were shopping. Doris was entertaining a couple of girl friends in the drug store. I wondered if they had seen Black Breed. Helen Maude had gone to Meridian with a bunch of teenagers. I sat shivering with George, Otho and Goober under the bandstand. The hair rose on our heads as we talked about the "boogy" man we had just seen.

"Black Breed's mighty big," George observed, "but Ah know a boy who swears he can hide behind somethin' as a liddle as a hoe handle."

"He has to be the meanest man that evah set foot in Newton County," Otho declared. "Pa says he keeps a long-barreled goose gun in his ole truck that can shoot an angel off a cloud."

"Yuh don't say," I murmured, not considering that Otho's daddy might be stretching facts a bit. "Wael, Ah'm nevah gonna go near 'um."

Little did I know that a couple of weeks later, I would come face to face with Black Breed during the most terrifying time of my life. It happened while I was down on the banks of Okahatta Creek, running my set poles and checking the trap line Uncle Semmy had showed me how to put down.

The traps were empty that day, but I caught a couple of good-sized channel catfish on set lines. I decided to call it a day and go home. My dog Sport had cut out earlier after a rabbit and had not returned.

I left the creek and took a short cut along an old stream bed leading into a pasture that had once been cleared for cattle grazing. The owner had sadly learned that only swamp grass would grow there due to the frequent flooding and had let it grow back to the wild.

I noticed an open spot in the high swamp grass at the edge of the dry stream bed. Coming closer, I saw a blade of grass slowly raise upright from its formerly flat position. I wanted to ask Uncle Semmy what could have stepped on the grass to flatten it out so, but my old woods pal had been gone now for almost a year.

Stepping back into the middle of the road, I dropped to one knee and carefully sighted across the mystery spot. Gradually, I made out the outline of a tire track in the bent grass. What was a vehicle doing down here?

I sighted ahead of the bent grass. Sure enough, another track.

The tracks led straight to a barbed wire fence — and through it! The marks were clearer now and I knew Uncle Semmy would be proud of me for my tracking skill.

My heart was thumping. I crept up to the wooden fence posts that stood to the right of the tire tracks. The mysterious intruder had cleverly cut the three strands of barbed wire and spliced wire at the ends to form loops around the fence post. This created a nifty gap in the fence through which a vehicle could pass when the wires were down. The wires had been drawn up tightly against the post to make it appear that there was no break in the fence.

Somebody had been back here in a car or truck not long ago!

Putting aside my fear, I dropped my stringer of fish on the grass and slipped between the wires. Following the mysterious tracks, I skirted the edge of the pasture that ran beside the old stream bed.

At one point I happened to glance up and spotted a freshly broken branch tip, a clear sign that something tall like a stake bed truck had passed this way. The leaves on the tip of the branch had only begun to wilt so I knew it had been broken quite recently.

About forty yards further on, the old stream bed looped out into the pasture. Expecting the tracks would continue to skirt the edge of the woods, I took a short cut down into the stream bed and crossed over to climb up a six-foot slope to the far side.

A darkening sky made the shadows seem all the more frightful. I wished for the company of George Snowden, or at least Sport. Unfortunately, George did not know where I was and Sport had evidently gone back to the farm.

Climbing up to the bushes, I pulled back a thick, leafy bush for a better view at the top.

I froze in horror!

Black Breed's eyes were staring straight into mine from no more than twenty feet away!

A shock like a bolt of electricity raced through my body so powerfully it caused my fingers and toes to tingle. I felt a jolt and then a stabbing pain in my chest. Black Breed and I stared at each other, he surprised and I frozen in fear.

My eyes in that brief instant recorded the whole operation of his moonshine still. He'd been squatting in front of his cooker feeding wood into a fire. His old Buick truck was parked off to the right, its stake bed half full with firewood. His copper cooker was a closed kettle with tell tale copper tubing coiling crazily upward. A metal container hung at the end of the tubing to catch the condensed alcohol. Leaning against the tree was that angel-shooting weapon, his long-barreled goose gun.

Suddenly in one swift movement, he pivoted on the balls of his feet, reached for his goose gun and lunged, hand outstretched toward me. Fear catapulted me into flight.

Surging up the opposite bank, I ran straight into a low hanging limb of a sweet gum tree. This slowed me almost to a standstill, and in that moment I could almost feel his clawing hands raking down my back. I spun and rolled out of the limb's embrace and heard his coarse oath as the limb sprang back against him.

When I reached the dirt road I dove head first between the strands of the barbed wire and ran as fast as I could toward my grandparents' house, three quarters of a mile away. I heard the barbed wires twang as Black Breed crashed into the fence, followed by a stream of profanity and heart-stopping threats:

"Boyah, yuh bettah not tay-ell, yuh bettah not tay-ell. Ah seen yuh an' iffen yuh tay-ell, Ah'll keeeel yuh."

Sprinting along the road, chest heaving, I pleaded over and over, "Oh, Jesus, please save me, please save me."

Some 200 yards on, I was crossing under the power line that ran over the road when I felt something wet and slimey brush against my legs. I was carrying my fish! Apparently, my hand had landed on and grasped my stringer when I dove through the fence. I flung the stringer to the side of the road. It landed in the path running under the high tension wires that bisected the road and led to Rattlesnake Lake. This instinctive gesture may have saved my life.

By now I was winded and my breath was coming in searing gasps. The pain under both sides of my ribs was almost intolerable and still I continued my terrorized flight.

Just beyond the power lines the road rose on the low red clay hill that ran by the piney woods. I staggered up the hill on rubber legs and trotted past an empty sharecrop house. Our house was now in view. Suddenly, I realized that I couldn't lead Black Breed there. Daddy Floyd was away in the fields and Grandmother, Helen Maude and Doris were in the house. In his anger at me, he might kill them too!

I swerved off the road, jumped the ditch and fell. Reeling to my feet I wobbled into the waist-high cotton field south of the house and ran dizzily down a contoured row which took me out of sight from the road.

My leaden legs collapsed under me. I had run flat out for three quarters of a mile and had absolutely no strength left. My breath came in piercingly painful gasps. My heart was racing out of control both from exertion and fear. A blinding pain roared through my head. Overalls soaked with sweat, I lay face down in the cotton field, chest heaving against the dirt.

The hysterical sobs came. There was no way to hold them back no matter how hard I tried. To suppress the sound so as not to draw Black Breed's attention, I pressed my mouth tightly into the crook of my arm. My body shook as I pictured Black Breed storming down the cotton row to snap my neck in his thick hands.

I didn't have the vigor to run anymore.

By the time I gained strength to stand again, the sun was dropping over the swamp. Seeing no sign of

Black Breed, I cautiously slipped to the end of the cotton row and wearily walked to our house.

"Jimmie, Ah been worried 'bout you," came Grandmother's voice from the darkened kitchen. What a sweet, safe sound.

"Why ah yuh so late gettin' home?"

"Ah jus' lost track of time, Grandmothah. Ah'm sorry if Ah worried you. Ah'll hurry up an' wash mah face."

I stepped across the darkened back porch and drew a bucket of cool water from the well. I could hear Grandmother bustling about in the kitchen, talking to Doris.

I whipped a wet wash cloth into the water to clean the tears and dirt off my face. Suddenly I lost control and burst into sobs again.

Grandmother was at my side in an instant, encircling me with her arms. "Jimmie, you'ah hot as fa'h. Ah yuh all right?"

"Yessum! Ah'm awl right. Ah jus' ran home an' got too warm."

She knew I wasn't telling all but she didn't press me. For some reason, neither did Doris.

"You'ah dirty an' sweaty, Jimmie. Go drag the wash tub up on the back poach. Doris, yuh go back to youah room. Ah'll get Jimmie some hot watah," Grandmother said, heading for the kitchen.

Grandmother scooped hot water from the reservoir on the wood cookstove in the kitchen and mixed it with cold water in the tub. She turned a coal oil lamp down low and placed it on the washstand beside the tub, but I quickly blew it out and bathed in the dark. I was afraid Black Breed was out there somewhere watching me. As I washed she draped my night shirt over the back of a chair outside the kitchen door and put a tall glass of buttermilk and corn bread on the kitchen table. After I dressed and sat down to eat I told myself I wouldn't tell a soul in the whole, wide world. I didn't dare tell. I was as afraid of Daddy Floyd killing Black Breed as I was of Black Breed killing me. I didn't want Daddy Floyd to be a murderer.

For the next four days I hung close to Grandmother and Daddy Floyd and anybody else who happened to be near. I never allowed myself to be alone, because my imagination placed Black Breed in one of the big walk-in closets, under a bed, in a wardrobe, the attic and anywhere else that evil might be lurking.

Each night, in my nightmares, I fought and ran from Black Breed over and over again. But I didn't tell. I didn't dare go back into the swamp. In fact, I left my poles still baited and my traps set along Okahatta Creek.

The following Wednesday I rode to town with Daddy Floyd, mainly to keep close to him. As we passed under the power line I saw tell-tale tire tracks at the edge of the road where a car had turned around. Or a Buick-turned-truck, maybe. I figured out what must have happened when Black Breed saw my abandoned fish. And I wondered if he had gone all the way up the power line path to Rattlesnake Lake. Shuddering a little, I inched closer to Daddy Floyd as he entered McCormack's Store.

Daddy Floyd struck up a conversation with Mr. McCormack. After awhile I got bored and shuffled to the door to look for a friend.

I had moved out on the sidewalk when a truck came rumbling down the street. Black Breed! Too paralyzed to run back in the store, I stood there transfixed.

Black Breed drove past and saw me! I hadn't dreamed he'd be in town on a week day. Usually, he made his moonshine whiskey sales on Saturday afternoon when all the field workers were in town.

Heart pounding, I quickly stepped around the corner of McCormack's and ran behind the shrubs in front of the Hickory Baptist Church. By the time Black Breed angled his truck into a parking place and had raced around the corner I was well hidden. Peering through the thick shrubbery, I saw his dark eyes sweeping up and down the line of shrubs, his lips silently mouthing the threat, "Ah'm, gon' keeeel yuh!"

After what seemed like an hour, he moved up Jackson Street, darting in and out of alleys, looking in and behind stores. I followed him nervously with my eyes, making sure not to blink, just as Uncle Semmy had taught me to do when we were watching squirrels.

Remaining hidden behind the shrubs, I finally saw Daddy Floyd come out of McCormack's with the spool of thread and sack of flour we had come to town to get for Grandmother.

Daddy Floyd did some socializing with several people under the shade canopy in front of a row of stores while I fretted. In ordinary times, I liked for him to chat with lots of people so I had more time to play. But today I just wanted to get out of town as fast as possible. When he was ready to go I saw his eyes searching for me across the square where I usually played when we went to town.

Black Breed had vanished when I ran across the street and quickly jumped in the car. I hunkered down below the lower part of the window so nobody could see me. Daddy Floyd looked at me kind of funny but didn't say anything. Not until he had driven out of town did I lift my head.

When I reached home a letter was waiting from Mother addressed directly to me. She wanted me to come to St. Louis in the middle of August. That was only two weeks before school was due to start. I had an uncanny feeling that I would be staying in St. Louis.

"What'd youah mothah's lettah say?" Grandmother asked.

"She wants me to come to St. Louis," I sniffed. "Ah don't want tuh leave yuh an' Daddy Floyd. All my friends ah heah. This is mah hoam." I choked back a sob.

Grandmother and Daddy Floyd read the letter carefully. "Wael," Daddy Floyd noted, "she's got a new house, Ah bet."

I laid my head on Grandmother's shoulder. "People ahn't friendly in St. Louis, like they ah heah. Ah wanna stay with yuh an' Daddy Floyd, an' Doris an' Helen Maude. Youah mah family. Mothah can come an' see me heah."

Daddy Floyd slipped an arm around my neck. "Jimmie, there's nothin' we'd like bettah. But youah mothah is a grown woman. We cain't tell her what to do. If she wants yuh with her, then that's wheah yuh belong. Ah'm shuah she'll let yuh come back foah visits."

I didn't tell Grandmother and Daddy Floyd that a part of me wanted to go where Black Breed couldn't find me.

Grandmother sent Mother my train schedule. On the appointed day they took me to the Meridian station to catch the Mobile & Ohio train for St. Louis.

A new era in my life was beginning.

Chapter 18

"A New Dad"

As my train pulled into St. Louis' Union Station on that memorable Saturday evening I pressed my face against the window, searching through the sea of faces on the platform. I caught sight of a slim hand waving above a blonde head. I mouthed the word: M O T H E R!

A distinguished looking man, dressed in suit and tie, was standing beside her. I was so happy to see Mother, that the relationship didn't connect until the train jolted to a stop and I saw them move as one toward my car.

I flew into Mother's arms. She hugged and kissed me and whirled me around to see the smiling stranger.

"Jimmie, this is Doctor Fritsch. Doctor O.J. Fritsch."

Mother hadn't said a word about him in a letter. I knew that he was my new daddy, but felt it impolite to ask. I merely extended my hand and said, "Pleased to meet yuh, suh."

Dr. Fritsch was less formal with me, slipping a soft hand on my shoulder. "Your mother has told me lots of good things about you, Jimmie. I'm looking forward to getting better acquainted." He spoke with a crisp, but friendly northern accent.

Dr. Fritsch got my bag. I trailed behind him and Mother as they led me to his car, a glistening new 1935 Ford.

He placed my bag in the back seat and I jumped in behind him and Mother. "Dr. Fritsch's an optometrist," Mother explained. "He checks people's eyes and fits them with glasses." Mother spoke almost like a Northerner.

Dr. Fritsch pulled away from the parking area. I had already noticed the rings on their hands, but still held back from asking The Question.

"We're goin' to our new apartment in University City," Mother said. "That's a real close-in suburb of St. Louis. It isn't far."

I thought of asking, "What's a suburb?" but didn't want to show my ignorance before Mother and my new dad.

"You'll love University City," Mother continued. "The school you'll be attending is one of the best in the country, and it's right across the street from where we live. We've already told them you'll be coming."

"Ah'm staying with yuh and goin' to school up heah?"

"Yes," Mother assured. "You'll live with us, then if your grandparents want you, you can visit them for the summer."

"Oh, theah'll want me," I assured Mother.

She still hadn't spoken the "M" word. It never occurred to me that they were living together out of wedlock. Respectable people didn't "shack up" in 1935.

Mother kept dancing around the subject until finally I could stand it no longer. "Mothah, ah yuh tryin' to tell me yuh an' Doctor Fritsch ah married?"

She blushed all colors. "Well, ah, yes, ah, I guess that's — No! that's what I am tryin' to say, Jimmie. I didn't tell you in my letter, for I wanted it to be a surprise."

She seemed astonished that I had concluded she was married, but she shouldn't have been. For years she had been telling me that some day she'd meet a nice man who would provide a home for us. Here we were in the middle of August and I'd moved north. What did she expect me to think? Mother's only son wasn't a super brain, but he was no dummy either.

Dr. Fritsch — it would take me all of three days before I started calling him, "Dad" — drove west through St. Louis and into University City to the Delmar Garden apartments. He and Mother had rented an apartment on the third floor, and the building had an elevator!

Mother took me up first and showed me around my new "home." Dr. Fritsch parked the car and then carried up my bag. He brought it into my room and he and Mother helped me put away my clothes in a brand new dresser.

Beyond the first time experience of having my own room, I was most impressed with their new console radio. Daddy Floyd and Grandmother still didn't have one. I had heard programs at the homes of friends in Hickory, but this was my first opportunity to fiddle with the dial as I pleased.

I was too tired to last long. Mother tucked me in bed and kissed me. "Goodnight, honey," she whispered. "You're home where you belong. Sleep tight and have pleasant dreams."

In the middle of that first night I had a nightmare. I was back in Hickory, hiding in the shrubbery from Black Breed. I heard his rough voice: "Ah'm gonna keeel yuh."

When I awoke, my heart was fluttering and the pillow case was soaked with sweat. Mother must have heard me moan. "Are you all right, Jimmie?" she called with some anxiety.

"Ah jus' had a bad dream," I assured her. "Ah'm okay now."

I fell back to sleep and had no more nightmares that night.

We slept in Sunday morning. Neither of them had said anything about going to church. After a leisurely late breakfast, "Dad" asked if I'd like to go for a drive. I gave an enthusiastic nod.

He drove south to Forest Park where the 1904 World's Fair had been staged. After looking around awhile, Dr. Fritsch took us to the riverfront where a big steamer had just arrived from New Orleans. We crossed the Eads Bridge into Illinois, then looped around and came back into Missouri across the Chain of Rocks Bridge. As we motored along, Dr. Fritsch and Mother kept up a running commentary about the sights and history of the area. Among many other things, Dr. Fritsch proudly told me that Lindbergh's epochal trans-Atlantic flight had been financed by St. Louis businessmen. "That's why his plane was called 'The Spirit of St. Louis,' " he said proudly.

After we returned to the apartment, I changed to my cut-offs and asked permission to walk around outside. I descended in the elevator to the lobby and stepped through the front door and out from under the marquee to the sidewalk.

"Yeooow!" The sidewalk was as hot as fire. I realized I'd have to begin wearing shoes on more than special occasions. I raced back to the elevator, shot upstairs, dashed into the apartment and hurriedly slipped on a pair of sneakers which Mother had bought for me to wear to school. Then I went back to the street and crossed to look around the deserted school playground.

I marveled at the prospect of a freed-up time schedule. On the farm, I had to be up for breakfast at six. Then Doris and I walked a mile to catch the school bus for a six-mile ride along dirt back roads, picking up other children. Here I could wake up half an hour before school started, enjoy breakfast without having to listen to catty remarks from Doris, ride a fancy elevator downstairs, and stroll across the street to school.

After supper we gathered around the radio to listen to Major Bowes and the Amateur Hour. I heard a girl "get the gong" which meant she wasn't good enough. I felt embarrassed and sorry for her and hoped her feelings weren't hurt too bad.

The characters on the Fred Allen show were absolutely hilarious. I tittered at Titus Moody's entrance line: "Hi yah, Bub." Titus said he'd only half slept the previous night because he had short eyelids.

I loved the Jewish lady on the show who responded to Fred Allen's, "Is that you, Mrs. Nussbaum?" with, "No. You expectin' maybe Hoagy Carmichael?"

Senator Claghorn's fakey, "Ah'm frum thuh South. Ah say pone an' 'possum," cracked me up. His accent sounded like a Northerner trying to talk like a Southerner.

I'd never heard anything so funny in all my life. They all talked so differently, with that clipped Northern tone. I never thought then that one day I'd talk just like them.

The next morning, Monday, Mother and Dad went off to work at their Delmar Loop Jewelry and Optical Shoppe on Enright Avenue. Mother managed the jewelry business and Dr. Fritsch, uh Dad, took care of the optical part, doing eye exams, ordering prescription lenses and custom grinding the lenses till they fit the shape of the frames that the customer had selected.

Left to my own devices on that first Monday morning, I rode the elevator downstairs and crossed the street to watch a half dozen boys batting a softball around. After awhile I noticed them glancing in my direction. When the dark-haired one they called Harold began walking toward me, I figured he was going to invite me to join their game. I was glad because I didn't have any friends yet and was beginning to feel lonesome.

Boy, was I in for a rude shock.

"Who are yah and whaddaya think you're lookin' at?"

I thought he must have mistaken me for some troublemaker.

"Ah'm Jimmie Rogers an' Ah jus' moved up from Mississippi," I answered, trying to smile.

"Yuh tryin' tuh get smart with me?" Harold demanded.

With that he slapped both hands against my chest and pushed hard. I'd have fallen down but the other boys had gathered around me in a circle and one of them pushed me back toward Harold.

Harold shoved me again and they all began pushing me back and forth in the middle of their circle, yelling "Hoosier! Stupid! Ugly Redhead!" and throwing in a few curse words to boot.

One gave me a granite stare. "Hoosiers hang colored people in Mississippi." The implication was that my life might be in danger.

"He's probably a Ku Klux Klanner," growled Harold.

"Ah'm not a Klan person," I protested. "Ah've nevah even seen a hangin'."

Harold and another boy slammed into me at once. "Yeah, yeah! That's what you say," Harold yelled.

I saw an opening in the circle and ran — as fast as I'd run trying to get away from Black Breed — across the street and into the lobby of the Delmar Garden complex.

They clustered under the marquee daring me to come out and threatening to beat me up and do other things that are too degrading for me to mention here. For the life of me I couldn't imagine what I'd done to offend them so terribly. If I'd known, I would have apologized to them at once. I finally had to leave the lobby and go upstairs before they would leave the front of the building.

I stayed in the apartment for a half hour or so and then took the elevator back downstairs and cautiously stepped out of the building. The boys were nowhere to be seen, so I walked down the street toward the larger Ward Junior High School. I'd barely reached the school on my left when two of the same boys dashed out from between two four-family flats on my right.

I ran into the alley and struck out for the Delmar apartments. Harold and another boy darted in from the street. I'd been staked out and was being run down like a rabbit.

Harold grabbed me roughly by the neck. "Thought you could get away from us, huh."

The rest caught up and surrounded me again. One pronounced himself "a judge" and ordered me taken to "jail."

Harold and the "judge" dragged me into the basement of one of the flats to a row of lockers. One hung open with a padlock hanging from the door handle. Harold and his cohorts pushed me in the locker and slammed the door behind my head.

"You're sentenced to stay here until somebody finds yah," the judge declared. "Ya might try screaming for help before ya pass out."

I heard footsteps echoing across the concrete floor. They were leaving me.

The locker was huge, eight by eight feet and built of boards. I didn't scream. After allowing time for them to get out of the building, I pulled out my scout knife and opened the screwdriver blade. It took only seconds to back out the screws that held the door hasp. I stepped out of the big locker and put the screws back in to reattach the hasp. Let them wonder how I escaped.

That "game" was repeated eight or nine times in the next three weeks. I'd be going somewhere and these urban hellions would jump me and lock me up. Fortunately, they never took my knife. Each time I took out the hasp screws and escaped.

Through all of these episodes I retained the ever diminishing hope that eventually I'd pass some sort of initiation and we could all be friends. The last straw came one day when they were chasing me down an alley. An overwhelming rage rose inside me. No human being, I vowed, should have to be run down like an animal.

I glanced over my shoulder and saw Harold leading the pack by twenty paces. I slowed down to let him get a little closer. He thought he was outrunning me and made an even greater effort. Reaching into my pocket as I ran, I grasped my knife in my right hand unopened and suddenly stopped.

Harold came rushing up. Whomp! I hurled my knife-clenched fist against his jaw.

He fell backward onto the alleyway. His head hit the ground and he was knocked out.

Never in my life had I hit anybody in rage and I felt good about it. I advanced in fury on Harold's gang members with clenched fists.

"C'mon, who'll be first. Come and get some of the same medicine Ah gave Harold. C'mon, c'mon," I taunted.

To my inexpressible delight, they began backing up. "Get some water on Harold," one shouted.

I stood by and watched while they pulled a hose from one of the four-family flats and squirted water on Harold. Pretty soon he sat up and started crying.

About this time an old Jewish lady came down the alley and started hollering at me, half in English and half in Yiddish. "Shame! Shame! God will judge you, young man. You're trying to hurt nice Jewish boys. You need counseling and help."

"Look, lady," I yelled back. If youah worryin' about 'nice' Jewish boys, you'd better start helping that'un on the ground."

It was heartless but I ignored the old woman and issued a warning to Harold: "If yuh evah see me comin' down the street again, yuh'd bettah pass over to the othah side."

The boys helped Harold up. He looked at me with fear and respect.

"Remembah," I warned, "you'd bettah stay out of mah way."

I turned and walked back to the apartment house. When Mother and Dad came home and asked about my day, I said, "Pretty good. Ah've been playin' with some of the neighbor boys."

The next week Mother formally enrolled me in the grade school across the street. I attended classes there every weekday, then played outside in good weather with other kids, including some members of Harold's gang. I usually went home when it was time for the radio adventure serials.

I sat alone listening to Tom Mix, yelling "yeah!" when he invited kids to be his "six-shooters." My heart skipped a beat when Little Orphan Annie opened with the sounds of a radio telegraph, steamboat whistle and a chugging locomotive. Jack Armstrong was my "All-American Boy." Captain Midnight sent chills up and down my spine. Then I heard a bustle in the hall and Mother and Dad came through the door.

Life fell into a kind of rhythm.

On weekdays Mother and Dad awakened me before they left for work. I ate cold cereal for breakfast, dressed and walked over to school. At the end of the school day I came home and changed clothes and played with other boys. As for Harold, when he saw me coming toward him, he always crossed the street. I got special satisfaction in that.

By five o'clock I was usually home listening to an adventure serial. At six my parents came home and Mother fixed dinner.

Saturdays, Mother and Dad worked until nine o'clock at night, leaving me to my own enterprises.

Sunday mornings we slept late, then in the afternoon Dad took us for a ride.

The weeks turned into months and before school was out I was looking forward to spending the summer on the farm. My only hesitancy was a fear of Black Breed that had never left me. Even in faraway St. Louis I continued to have nightmares of him chasing me.

The day after school was out, Mother and Dad put me on the train. Daddy Floyd, Grandmother, Doris and a grown-up, eighteen-year-old Helen Maude met me at the Meridian station.

When I returned Goober Brown came out to see me. "Did yuh heah, Jimmie? Black Breed come up missin' right aftah yuh left foah Saint Louie. They foun' his ole Buick truck down by Potterchitto Creek but he was nowheah tuh be seen."

I had never told anyone about Black Breed chasing me out of the swamp. It didn't seem safe to comment one way or the other to Goober. As long as Black Breed's body hadn't been found I couldn't be sure he was dead. I didn't want to think about the feared outlaw, so I thrust him further into the back recesses of my mind. I heard rumors about black fathers who didn't like the cruel ways their daughters had been abused by Black Breed. A story also circulated about the bootlegger whose arms he had broken and one about two others he had scared out of "cookin' up" whiskey. But nobody ever presented proof that Black Breed was dead. I listened and kept my mouth shut.

So ended the most frightening year of my young life. I'd come face to face with my own mortality and the reality that I could actually die. It was more of a burden than an eleven year old should have had to bear.

It was over a half a century later and only after I decided to write about my boyhood that I could bring the memory to the surface and tell my wife, Laura, about Black Breed's pursuit. And then to write it down. This helped—even after all those years.

Chapter 19

"Bees in the Church"

I was back in Mississippi for the summer of 1939, helping Daddy Floyd on the farm. "Let's take a run into Hickory for some wire to fix the fence in the lower paschah," my grandfather said.

Daddy Floyd dropped me at the hardware store to pick up a roll of barbed wire while he drove over to McGee's mill for some corn meal.

As I came out with the wire, a familiar voice caught my ear.

"Hey, city boy, how long yuh been back from Saint Louie?"

I turned to see Edwin Johnson. It had been years since Edwin and his prankish brothers took me snipe hunting and their daddy whipped them because he thought they'd left me to get lost in the woods. I decided to let bygones be bygones and act as if the incident had never happened.

"Oh, Ah reckon Ah been heah 'bout two weeks now," I drawled, affecting more of an accent than I still retained.

Edwin kicked at a stray dog that came idling by. "Say, Jimmie, mah brothers an' me's goin' over to Newton tomorrah night. Ya wanna come 'long?"

Newton was about seven miles west of Hickory. A Baptist junior college was there which Grandmother hoped I might attend some day.

"Whatcha gonna do in Newton?" I asked Edwin.

"Oh, theah's always sumthin' excitin' goin' on in Newton," said Edwin.

I thought for a moment and decided. "Nah, Ah reckon Ah bettuh not. Ah don't have any transportation."

"Oh, we'll come 'n gitcha," responded Edwin quickly—too quickly, I reflected later.

"Well, awright, what time?"

"Be ready 'bout six an' mah brothas an' me'll pick yuh up."

When Daddy Floyd came to get me at the store, I told him I was thinking of going over to Newton with the Johnson boys the next night. He didn't answer me, but just kept driving toward home. I figured he hadn't heard me above the roar of the engine. I didn't repeat the comment while we were working on the fence that afternoon. When we finished we put away the tools in the shop and were walking to the house when from out of the blue Daddy Floyd spoke:

"Yuh know, Jimmie, when yuh run aroun' with a circle of fools, soon'ah or latah you'ah gonna fin' youahsef in the middle of the circle with them fools pointin' at yuh."

He talked almost in riddles sometimes, especially when he was trying to get me to think twice about something. If I asked him what he meant, he usually answered, "Jus' think about it."

That's what he said this time. He didn't say I couldn't go. He just said, "Think about it."

I thought about it and still didn't get his message.

The Johnson boys drove up about fifteen minutes after supper the next evening. I sensed an air of excitement the moment I stepped into the car. Tom was driving his Daddy's 1936 two-door Ford sedan and Harley sat next to him. Edwin and Billy Joe perched in the back seat and I squeezed in between them. Between us was a large round object covered with cloth, which I didn't ask about and would have saved myself a lot of trouble if I had.

Tom pulled slowly away from the house. Looking out the back window, I saw Daddy Floyd step off the front porch and follow out into the road to watch as the car rolled down the red clay hill towards the Oakhatta Creek swamp. Strange, I thought. Daddy Floyd had never done that before when I was going somewhere.

As soon as Tom dropped down the low hill to the swamp he picked up speed, sliding the rear wheels around at every turn. I knew he was a good driver but I wished he wouldn't drive quite so reckless.

When Tom reached the highway he pulled back a knob to open the cutout. That allowed the exhaust to by-pass the muffler, giving the Ford even more power and speed. He floored the accelerator and in no time at all we were flashing along at eighty miles an hour! Not accustomed to riding so fast, I was scared. But I didn't protest. I didn't want to be called a sissy.

Edwin tapped on Tom's shoulder and signaled for him to close the cutout. When the noise died down Edwin told me that the engine had special work done to it to make the car run faster. He claimed that the modified 1936 two-door Ford sedan was the fastest and best balanced car on the road and was the first choice of bootleggers. I wondered why that was so important to him, but I didn't ask. Listening to the souped up engine and hearing the wind whistling put my nerves on edge. I didn't doubt that I was in a fast car—a very fast car.

As we approached Hickory, Tom turned to his brother, Harley. "Be careful that stopper don't come outta the jug, oah we'll all be in a heap of trouble."

This comment brought peals of laughter and I asked what was so funny, but they wouldn't tell me. I worried now that the jug, wrapped in a white flour sack, might contain moonshine. If the sheriff stopped us, we'd be in a peck of trouble.

"Jus' wait, Jimmie," Tom said. "It'll be moah fun foah yuh if it's a suhprise."

Again, the brothers laughed and I wondered what I was getting into.

Tom pulled into the filling station at the corner of U.S. Highway 80 and State Highway 503 in Hickory to get gas and to buy some cigarettes. Tom went inside and talked to Wendell Bailey, a friend of his. They were laughing and cutting up and at one point Tom jerked his thumb over his shoulder toward the car. Wendell came to the door of the station and I had the feeling he was trying to get a better look at me. He shook his head and slapped Tom on the shoulder and they both started laughing again.

As we zipped on toward Newton, I noticed that every two or three minutes Harley would give the glass jug a little shake. I couldn't see what was in the jug because of the wrap around it. All I saw was the glass neck and a corn cob stuck in the top with a long string wound around it.

Tom turned halfway around toward me in the driver's seat. "We'ah gonna go to church tonight, Jimmie."

His three brothers absolutely broke up with laughter but I didn't see anything so funny about going to church. When we reached Newton, Tom didn't stop but drove all the way through town. Just beyond where the road turned to gravel he switched off the car lights and engine and began coasting.

"We'ah almost theah," he whispered. "Evahbody be real quiet an' don't slam the car doors when yuh get out."

As Tom turned and rolled silently down a dirt driveway, the sound of singing and shouting reached our ears. "Theah's the church," Harley whispered.

The car coasted past horses, buggies, wagons and a few cars, coming to a stop in the driveway behind the building.

"Why ah we stoppin'—?"

Edwin and Billy Joe grabbed me fiercely, clamping hard hands over my mouth, while Tom whirled around in his seat and growled hoarsely, "Shut up, Jimmie, do yuh wanna spoil the fun?"

I hoped the fun would start soon because up to now with my mouth clamped shut and Tom glaring at me, I hadn't been having much.

"Get out uv the car, Jimmie," Tom whispered in my ear, "Slip 'round to the front uv the church an' watch out foah me. Don't let anybody see yuh."

As I left, I noticed the four brothers placing a ladder against the back wall of the church just under the middle of three windows high upon the back wall. I guessed the ladder had been left on the ground back there.

I kept my head down and ran toward the front. Inside I could hear hands clapping, feet stamping and shouts of "Praise the Lord!" I figured it must be a Full Gospel Church.

I stood at the front for a minute or two, wondering what I was supposed to be watching for and why I shouldn't be seen. I wanted to do a good job for Tom, so I quickly ran back to the rear of the church to ask him. When I silently approached the darkened car I heard Edwin ask Tom, "Yuh think Jimmie knows anything'?"

Tom cackled in the dark. "Nah, Jimmie's too dumb to catch on."

Watching from the shadows, I saw all the boys except Harley jump in the car. Tom started the engine, leaving the passenger side door open for Harley. I still didn't understand what was going on but an uneasiness in my gut made me hang back. From my position in the shadows I ran my eyes up to the top of the ladder and saw Harley with the glass jug, just under the opened window.

Harley had tied the end of a string to the top of the ladder and removed the strip of flour sack from around the jug. A window screen lay on the ground near the bottom of the ladder. I looked up at Harley and in that instant I realized what they had planned for me.

Harley was grinning wickedly and shaking the jug with a vengeance. The light from the windows revealed what was inside. The jug was full to the top with mad bees!

Here, miles from home, the Johnson boys were about to make me the fall guy for the most stupid prank ever pulled in Newton County.

Harley was going to drop that jug full of angry bees behind the preacher and when it broke there'd be some hallelujah people leaving real fast. They'd see me at the front and peg me as the disturber of their worship. The string, I figured, was for insurance in case the jug didn't break. But it wasn't needed because when the jug fell it broke into a zillion pieces.

Suddenly I remembered Daddy Floyd's words about running around with a circle of fools and me being in the middle. And here I was smack dab in the middle! This was to be the payback for what I'd done to the Johnson boys on that snipe hunt three years before. They hadn't forgotten my coup and their daddy's whipping, as I'd hoped, but had waited for the opportunity to get sweet revenge.

Feet do your stuff.

I whirled around, flew back to the front of the church, jumped the ditch that ran alongside the street and raced down the road in terror toward Newton. In the night blackness, a souped-up engine roared to life and I knew that Tom and his brothers would be "moaning low" toward Hickory without me, right according to plan.

I glanced back over my shoulder and in spite of my fear, stopped right in the middle of the road and watched the most amazing sight I'd ever seen. People were pouring out of the church swinging and swatting and hollering. They raced out the front door, the side door and soared through the open windows — even the closed windows — like a human waterfall!

Then the bees spread out from the church to launch their second wave of attack. The whinnying horses and mules bucked and jumped, trying to escape their traces. The whole scene was madness personified.

Some of the men pointed up the road toward the dust cloud under the street light that Tom had churned up, and ran to get their cars. Knowing the chance I took if I was caught, I cupped my hands around my mouth and shouted as loud as I could, "It was the Johnson boys from Hickory that done it! Tom Johnson and his brothers from Hickory!"

Eyes turned toward where I stood unseen in the dark. So far, I'd been lucky but Daddy Floyd had seen me leave with the Johnson boys and I'd need a rock-solid alibi to get myself out of trouble when he heard about the breakup of the church service. I ran as fast as I could toward the business section of Newton, hoping nobody could hear my heavy breathing.

Up the street I saw a possible solution to my problem: Ray McGee's Dad's 1939 Chevrolet, parked in front of the Newton Theater where a cowboy movie was playing. I was sure the car belonged to Ray's dad. I walked up to the little box office, bought a ticket and entered. As my eyes adjusted to the dark, I scanned the rows of seats for Ray.

Sure enough, there Roy sat with Otho Harris and Sookie Adams right up in the first row in the best seats—where you could lay your head back and your neck never got tired. Their eyes were fixed on the screen where the sheriff was chasing a bank robber wearing a bandanna over the lower part of his face.

I slipped up to that row and bent over and whispered, "Ray? Is that you? Ah've been lookin' all ovah foah yuh."

"Jimmie, whut in Sam Hill ah yuh doin' heah?"

"Ah hitched a ride ovah. Can Ah ride home with yuh?"

When he said yes, my cast iron alibi was set. Now all I had to do was keep an innocent face and avoid being put in the position of having to answer a direct question from Daddy Floyd. I didn't think I could lie to my grandfather while he looked me in the eye.

I sat through the rest of the show, then walked with Ray, Otho and Sookie to the car. When we reached Hickory I asked Ray to stop at J.B. Fanning's filling station where I insisted on buying him some gas. While J.B. was putting the gas in the car, he asked us if we had heard about "all the excitement."

"Nah," Ray said, "we were at the show in Newton."

"You should have been here," J.B. said. "A '36 two-door Ford shot through town like a bullet with its cutout wide open. Must have been goin' at least a hundred mile' an houah. The sheriff was chasing it, but I don't think he evah caught up. Looked like Mr. Amos Johnson's car from tow'd Newton way.

I asked J.B. about his wife Hazel's health and said I was real glad to see him. Boy! My alibi was getting better all the time. Ray got me home about twelve o'clock and Daddy Floyd came outside on the porch while I was saying good night to Ray—loudly.

"That was Ray McGee, wasn't it?"

I tried to appear startled. "Oh, I didn't see yuh, Daddy Floyd. Yessuh, that was Ray."

Before he could ask me any more questions, I told him that I'd gotten out of the Johnsons' car in Newton, which I had, and gone to the picture show, which I also had, and Ray had brought me home. "Uh, huh," Daddy Floyd responded. "Ah'm goin' back to bed."

I stayed outside in the yard for a little while to watch the moon rising over the tall swamp trees near the piney grove. I thanked more than my lucky stars for delivering me from the punishment which the Johnson boys had intended.

Daddy Floyd and I went into Hickory the next day and found the whole town buzzing! Daddy Floyd heard the news from Ray's uncle at the grist mill, about how somebody had dumped a jug of bees into the Full Gospel Church at Newton. Daddy Floyd was furious that somebody would do such a thing. He was a Baptist but he took it as a personal affront that anybody would do this to any church.

"Jimmie," he said, "Ah bet those Johnson boys had somethin' to do with this. You'ah lucky yuh left them last night an' went to the picture show."

"Yessuh, Ah'm sho glad Ah got a ride back with Ray. Ah'm not goin' to have any truck with them Johnson boys any moah."

And I didn't.

But whether I associated with them or not their pranks continued. The next year, just before Halloween, Mr. Johnson told Tom to return a large boom truck to a place down south in Jasper County. Mr. Johnson had rented the boom truck to swing some big timbers out over a bridge he was building over Potterchitto Creek in the south part of Newton County.

Tom got his brothers to go with him. Instead of going south, Tom swung north up Decatur Road a few miles and drove out to the Widow Hawkins' place. The Johnson boys knew Widow Hawkins was hard of hearing so Tom pulled up almost to her barn and Edwin and Billy Joe led her milk cow up to the fence.

Tom and Harley had made a big sling which they looped under the old cow and hoisted her right over the fence. They drove down the road to the grade school with the cow still chewing her cud while swinging from the boom behind the truck.

Tom switched off the lights and drove in back of the school where they hoisted the cow to the roof. Then Tom dropped his brothers off and drove on to Jasper County to return the truck.

When the sun came up the next day, there was the Widow Hawkins' cow on the school roof chewing her cud and looking as contented as could be. Everybody came out to give advice on how to get her down. In the end the principal had the county road supervisor bring a boom truck to lower the big animal down to earth.

Nobody ever proved that the Johnson Boys actually did this, but everybody figured it had to be them. Many people thought it was funny but they couldn't approve of the shenanigan for fear their own sons would copy the Johnson boys.

The "last straw" came during the Christmas holidays of the following year when the Johnson boys decided to "get" a school principal for kicking a friend out of school in Jasper County, which adjoined Newton County on the south. The Johnsons had never developed a deep fondness for education and without even knowing what the boy had done, they sided with him.

To start with, the four incorrigibles pulled off a night-time chicken heist at a farm near Hickory. Loading the chickens and a hundred-pound sack of feed into their dad's pickup, they drove down to the high school in Jasper County.

They backed up to the principal's office, pried open the window, and dropped in 200 lively birds. Then they poured the chicken feed on the office floor and put a five gallon bucket of water in the room. Their dastardly deed down, they drove away laughing with glee.

Goober Brown told me about the escapade a couple of summers later. I started to grin and he begged, "Please don't laugh, Jimmie. It wadden funny, not one bit. If it had been foah one day it might have been funny. If it had been foah only two days, it might have been hilarious, but it was foah two weeks, through Christmas and New Years, an' it wuz jus' awful. Them chickens gobbled up that chicken feed an' processed the whole hundred pounds of it an' the mess wuz jus'—jus'—evah'wheah. The principal's wife," he added, had "saved foah most 'bout two years to buy him a real leathah swivel chair an' it was purely ruint."

Goober stopped and waited for the full effect of this news to sink in on me. Then he continued.

"The principal let evahbody come an' jus' look foah themselves. Nobody a'tall laughed. It wuz that bad, Jimmie. The principal's wife worked her fingers to the bone, tryin' tuh scrub that chicken crud out of the leathah chair but it wuz no use."

By now the story had taken on a completely different flavor and I didn't see any humor in it at all.

"Did the Johnson boys evah get caught?" I asked. "They oughta go to the penitentiary for that."

"Well, the Jasper County sheriff come ovah heah an' questioned them boys ovah an' ovah but they nevah did confess."

"Then, close to March, alluva sudden they wuz gone! I wuz down at Simpson's Stoah late one night gettin' Pa some chewin' tobaccah, when Mr. Johnson come in with two trucks and his car loaded with eveahthing they owned. They gassed up an' headed down State 503, but fo' they left the fillin' station Edwin Johnson whispered the whole story to me, like he wuz proud of it. That's how Ah know to tell it to yuh.

"We heard that all the school children down in Jasper County took up a collection to buy anothah chair foah the principal but Ah don't spec' it meant as much as the one his wife bought him."

"Does anybody know where the Johnsons went?" I asked Goober.

"If they do, they ain't talkin'."

Somehow our whole county, and I expect Jasper County too, felt a lot safer.

Chapter 20

"The Great Treasure Hunt"

Later in the summer, after my narrow escape at the Full Gospel Church, I tagged along with Daddy Floyd on a trip to McGee's grist mill. Ray came running over to see me. From the way he spoke, I could tell he had something on his mind.

"Hey, Jimmie, yuh gotta come out an' spend Friday night with me. Goobah Brown is comin' an' bringin' a treasuah map."

I didn't catch the word "treasuah" before map, maybe because I'd always thought Goober was a little too slick.

I shrugged and looked over at Daddy Floyd, who was pulling out the sack of corn. He didn't see "why not," so long as I was back by Saturday night and ready for church the next morning.

Ray lived in Hickory and I couldn't catch a ride there. I ended up walking the three miles from the farm on Friday afternoon. Goober was there when I arrived.

"How yuh doin', ole pal?" Goober greeted me like I was a long lost brother. I should have suspected something then, but Ray's mother interrupted with a call to supper. "Yuh jus' got heah in time," she informed me with a smile.

After the meal Ray hustled us into his bedroom and closed the door, acting very mysterious.

"All right, Goobah, show Jimmie the map."

I stayed quiet, not having the slightest idea of what Ray was talking about.

Goober looked hesitant and said, "Ah, don't know, Ray. Did yuh sweah him to secrecy?"

Ray was short tempered and I saw his face turn red. I didn't want to get him started, so I said to Goober, "Ah sweah, Goobah"—not having the slightest idea what I was swearing to.

Goober shifted his eyes around the bedroom, got down on his knees and pretended to look under the bed while Ray rolled his eyes in impatience.

"Show 'im the map Goobah, fo' Ah get mad!"

Goober reached inside his shirt and withdrew a crumpled piece of brown paper, with some writing and lines on it.

He whispered in a dramatic voice. "This is the secret treasuah map."

Long silence greeted his revelation, while I looked bewildered. Finally I said, "That jus' looks like a piece of groc'ry sack."

"Why, Jimmie whatta yuh mean? Ah yuh an expert on treasuah maps?" Ray demanded to know.

I was not buying. "Evah 'body tha's got a lick of sense knows papuh turns brown when it gets old. 'Sides, evah 'body in Newton County has heard that ole Juzan Lake story. I heard it ag'in jus' a couple of nights ago from Noel Skinner who happens to be the grandson of Mistuh Juzan. Noel says when his gran'daddy heard the Yankees were comin', he drove his buggy into the lake, carryin' the gold wrapped in deerskins. Accordin' to Noel, his gran'daddy shot the hoss and swum to the bank, leavin' the buggy to sink in eighty foot of watah. Then he and his wife headed foah New Orleans. Noel says people have drug the lake with hooks a hundred times, tryin' to get his gran'daddy's treasuh'. All they evah pulled out was ole dead tree limbs."

"Jimmie, we'ah not talkin' 'bout that ole Juzan tale," Ray informed me impatiently. "This is anuthah treasuh. Ain't nobody 'roun' heah evah heard of it. It was buried out in the swamp by Confederate soldiers. Goobah jus' found the map in an ole trunk passed down by his grandmothah.."

The mystery and intrigue heightened. Maybe they were really on to something.

We sat there in Ray's room and examined the "map" on the thick brown paper. I couldn't make anything out of it, but the strangest thing happened. I began to believe it really was a treasure map. Listening to Goober and Ray talk about what they were going to buy with their shares, I began buying things in my mind.

Soon it was dark enough that nobody could see us. We couldn't be too careful when so many millions of dollars in gold were at stake. Searching through Ray's garage, we found a shovel and a pick axe and, with Ray carrying a lantern, we started walking down the railroad tracks toward Chunky,

243

carrying our lanterns and treasure-digging tools. We'd walked over two miles when Goober suddenly stopped and held up his hand.

"We hafta turn heah."

Following Goober, we hiked across an open field for what must have been a half mile, and finally came to the banks of the Potterchitto Creek southeast of Hickory. Goober paced back and forth as I became increasingly excited.

"Dig heah," he finally announced and I flew to the task.

I dug until I was out of breath and then Ray took over. He dug furiously for a time and handed the shovel to Goober, gasping, "How much deepah?"

Goober sat down close to the lantern and added and subtracted some numbers on the edge of the map. He then handed the shovel to me, whispering knowingly, "Not much moah."

"Not much moah" meant we were almost on top of all that gold and silver. I could almost feel the rare gold coins trickle through my fingers and clink as they fell on the big pile. I imagined myself saying to all the newspaper reporters who would be coming:

"Well, now that Ah'm a millionaire, Ah don't hafta go to school no moah up north, an' all Ah gotta do is jus' lay aroun' an' drink Orange Crush an' eat hambugahs. Heah's the keys to mah new Cadillac. Why don't you felluhs try it out an' see how you like it. Don't worry none 'bout scratchin' it 'cause if yuh do, Ah'll jus buy me anothuh one."

Delicious thoughts! Greed had completely enslaved me and I dug so furiously I thought my arms were going to fall off. Soon I threw the shovel down and choked out in breathless exhaustion, "Wheah is it, Goobah?"

Goober took the shovel and passed it to Ray. "Heah, boy, yuh can shovel fo' a minnit whilst Ah check the map again."

Ray started to dig more slowly. Goober looked up from the map at him. "Ray, the way Ah figgah it, we can't be ovah six inches away from paydirt. Maybe you'll be the one that hits all that gold first."

Well that did it. At the thought that he'd be able to say he was actually the one who dug the treasure up, Ray started shoveling like a madman. To save him from falling over, I suggested that he let me shovel for awhile. "Ah'm not neah 'bouts as tired as I thought a minute ago." But he glared at me and kept going like a house afire until he collapsed and fell over flat on his back.

Ray lay on the ground wheezing for a long time and then, reaching for the map, said huskily, "Lemme see that ole papah, Goobah."

Goober handed him the mysterious document. Ray examined the lines very carefully.

"This stupid map don't make no sense atall," he mumbled.

Then he turned the map over and knelt down to hold it closer to the lantern on the ground. Suddenly he jerked bolt upright and almost shouted.

"Goobah, the back of this map's got printin' on it that says P-I-G-G-L—Hey! This ain't no seventy-yeah ole map cause it's drawed on a Piggly Wiggly groc'ry stoah sack."

Ray grabbed up the shovel and advanced menacingly on Goober with the shovel drawn back. Later, when Ray had recovered his sanity, we speculated that Goober must have first been taken in by his older brother who had given him the map. And I'm sure Goober could have reasoned with Ray—about a month later. Right now, Goober wanted to grow up, get married to a pretty little girl, and reach for the American dream—even without all that Confederate gold. Looking into Ray McGee's angry eyes in the flickering lantern light, he wasn't so sure he was going to make it.

"Now lissen, Ray, lissen to me—"

But it was all too obvious that Ray wasn't going to listen to anybody. Ray had been taken in and he was decidedly unhappy about it.

Goober turned to me with a desperate look in his eyes but no sniveling appeal could compensate for my shattered dreams. I wasn't going to be interviewed by all those reporters, after all. No gold coins were going to trickle through my fingers. I'd have to work hard for every Orange Crush I'd ever drink. I'd have to finish school and be dirt poor all the rest of my life. And it was all that deceivin' Goober's fault!

Goober saw me reach for the pick ax. He turned tail and ran like a chicken thief with Ray and me in hot pursuit.

We chased him all the way to the railroad tracks and then lost him. We figured he must have hid out on the other side of the elevated road bed and then slunk down the tracks toward Chunky, six miles to the east.

Ray and I shuffled back toward Hickory in silence. After awhile, I reminded him. "Well we still got owah health, anyway."

Ray glared at me fiercely and I didn't say any more.

I stayed with Ray that night and walked back to the farm the next morning.

Daddy Floyd was making a window frame in his shop. He heard Sport bark and came to the door. "You came back soonah than ah expected," he said. "Yuh look plumb tuckered out."

I nodded.

"Go ask your grandmother for a glass of cool, sweet milk. That'll put vigah in youah bones." Daddy Floyd laughed and turned back to his work.

Sunday morning and night we went to church where for three years I'd been sitting on the Brothers' side. Daddy Floyd saw me squirming in the pew and asked if anything was the matter. I straightened my shoulders and shook my head.

I did a lot of thinking about myself that week. About hitting the Jewish boy, Harold, in University City and feeling good about it. About all the mean things I'd said to Aunt Doris over the years. About deceiving Daddy Floyd regarding the trip to Newton when Harley Johnson dropped the jug of bees into the church. About my greediness in thinking how Goober's "gold" would make me rich.

I thought about my Uncle Lamar dying at four. The Lord had let me live to twelve. Maybe I'd die before another birthday. Maybe I'd be killed in a train wreck on the way back to St. Louis. Maybe Harold or one of his friends would shoot me when I got back.

I was not at peace with myself and God.

There had been times at church when I'd seen people stream forward to answer the preacher's invitation to "come and be saved."

"Why ah they goin' up theah?" I'd ask Grandmother.

"Theah answering God's call to accept Jesus and be saved," she'd say.

"How will Ah know when Ah get God's call?

"You'll know, you'll know," she always said assuringly.

August came with smoldering heat. Revival time at Hickory Church. We went every night. Without air conditioning, the sweat steamed our faces. A hundred cardboard funeral home fans kept the fresh air circulating that blew in through the windows.

We sat together as families for the revival. Each night as the preacher extended the altar call, I sensed my grandparents' eyes on me. I knew they would have pushed me down the aisle if that had been sufficient. But they could not hasten God's work.

The last night came. The preacher finished his sermon and held out his arms. "Come to Jesus," he pleaded. "Come tonight. There may never be another time like this for you to be saved."

"Just as I am, without one plea; but that Thy blood was shed for me..." the people sang.

I waited to feel a compulsion, a divine shove, so to speak. I saw others going to the altar. I wanted to feel as they felt. I wanted the assurance that my sins were forgiven. I sensed Grandmother and Daddy Floyd's agitation. They so much wanted me to "accept the Lord."

They sang the last stanza of "Just as I am." Head hanging from my own misery, I waited for the preacher to announce the names of those who had been saved.

Instead, he said, "Brothahs and sistahs, let's sing the first stanza one moah time. I have the feelin' theah's somebody heah who God is calling, someone who's holding back. Come, come, come, while we sing."

I stared at my feet.

"Just as I am, without one plea; but that Thy blood was shed for me. And that Thou bid'st me come to thee, O Lamb of God, I come, I come."

"What's keeping me from going to the altar?" I wondered — and then I noticed my feet were moving.

I looked up to see the prayer railing before me. Suddenly Daddy Floyd was on one side and Grandmother on the other. Both were in a delirium of tears and I joined them.

I was baptized along with the other new Christians in the Hickory Church baptistry. The next week I took the train back to St. Louis. I rushed into Mother's open arms and heard her "welcome home," while Dad Fritsch stood by grinning, "It's good to have you back, Jimmie."

In Care of the Conductor

As we drove away from Union Station, I felt at peace with God and man. I was with parents who loved me. New adventures and a new school year lay ahead. When the school term ended, I'd go back to spend another summer with Daddy Floyd and Grandmother on the farm.

What more could a boy want?

Afterword

"Backward, turn backward, O Time in your flight'
Make me a child again just for tonight."
— Elizabeth Akers Allen

Almost sixty years have passed since I roamed the fields and swamps of Newton County, Mississippi. Years that have flown "swifter than a weaver's shuttle" (Job 7:6).

Years of change in the lives of loved ones who peopled my youth of long ago.

Should you be interested, here's what happened to my nearest and dearest:

Aunt Doris, my "sibling rival," grew up and married Roy Elmore. Roy loved her faithfully until the day he died. They produced two fine sons, Richard Leroy and Mark Rush, and a daughter, Debra Jean, known affectionately as D.J..

Doris and I came to understand one another better as we got older. We found we could actually laugh about painful incidents of days gone by.

Helen Maude, the aunt who could find no fault in me, married a man from Philadelphia, Mississippi. I liked him very much, but alcohol destroyed their marriage.

Aunt Helen faced much pain in her life, both physical and emotional. Most of her pain was eased by being given, through adoption, a baby she named Kim. After her divorce, she moved to Jackson where she worked two jobs to put her dear Kim through Mississippi State University.

I remember my beloved "Hey-Maude" as loyal, loving, kind and soft-spoken. When my grandparents and mother died, I hurt but I didn't cry. When Helen Maude died I was in my fifties, and I cried.

Vernell was the wilder of my two uncles and had wanderlust. He left home to travel through Louisiana doing contract plowing, but after a while he became homesick and returned. He met a girl named Angie Griffths over in Chunky and brought her back to the farm as his wife. Grandmother became her second mother, even to the point of teaching her good grammar.

Nell and Angie bought a used 1923, hard-top, Model T Ford, four-door sedan for $35 — about three weeks wages back then. Nell did some engine repairs and took off for Akron, Ohio.

Sadly, Nell and Angie split up. Nell moped around a while, then when life seemed darkest, he began seeing Angie's sister, Mary Alice. They married a year or so later, had two fine sons, Tim and Jeff, and a daughter, Jennell and lived in Akron where Nell died.

Cecil (Brothah) married a Newton County girl named Winnie Harris. To Brothah's keen disappointment, he and Winnie never had any children of their own. I was the nearest he ever came to having a son.

Daddy Floyd continued to be greatly respected in the entire area, by both white and black people. When he passed away in 1962 at the age of eighty-one, many of his friends and admirers came home to Hickory to pay their respects. One black man came from Chicago and another arrived from California.

When someone suggested to Grandmother that the black people should wait until the white people had viewed the body first, she spoke quietly, but with firm indignation.

"No! Floyd wouldn't want that an' Ah don't want it either! Let fokes get in line as they come."

It required over two hours for the line to pass his casket.

After Daddy Floyd died, Grandmother lost her fear of driving fast in a car, and miracle of miracles, began to travel on airplanes.

I don't think she had a death wish but I know she longed to be with her beloved "Floyd." She told me once that as soon as she got to Heaven she was going to ask to see Jesus. Next she would look for her husband. Then she said, "An', Jimmie, Ah'll want to talk to [the Apostle] Paul b'cause Ah nevah did undahstand evah one of those things he wrote about."

Grandmother joined her heart-mate and life-mate in 1971.

I could write a whole book about my brave mother. When she married Dr. Fritsch, he was barely eking out a living from his jewelry store. She marched into the store, cleaned up the place, converted stacks of jewelry into displays, painted on a confident smile, ignored the depression, and turned the business into a huge financial success. In fact, the business prospered so much that she and Dad purchased a very nice home in Romona Hills, a suburb of St. Louis. Thanks to Mother and Dad, I was one of only three boys in my high school to have a convertible. It sure beat riding the school bus along the back roads of Newton County, Mississippi.

Dad Fritsch filled the empty place in my heart, and it felt good as I had anticipated. But there was still a shoe hanging there — needing to drop. I knew from an early age that I would have to search for my birth father — the one whom I had once dreamed would come for me at Daddy Floyd and Grandmother's.

I attended the schools in University City, left to enter the Navy in 1942 and then married in 1943 at the age of nineteen. After World War II ended, I sailed as a Merchant Seaman for two more years before coming home in 1948 to settle down with my wife and four-year-old son, Keith. Daughter Carolyn arrived in 1949 and Eric followed quickly in 1950. Any thoughts of searching for my birth father had been put off by the demands of getting a decent-paying job and providing a home for my family.

I took my family to visit my grandparents in July of 1952 and after we left we waved our "Goodbyes" until we dropped down the hill past the piney woods into the shadows of the swamp road. From the point where we entered the low part of the swamp road until we emerged at Highway 80, three-quarters of a mile away, I completed plans on how to locate my birth father, the man who lay in the arms of another woman on the night I was born.

At the time the only information I had was the name of a garage in Vicksburg, Mississippi, where he had worked twenty-seven years before, and the name of another mechanic in that shop, Hosie Hester.

God must surely protect the helpless through stupidity, because I loaded in my wife and children and traced that man through four jobs in Mississippi and Louisiana to Kilgore, Texas. By the time we reached Kilgore we were exhausted. It was over 100 degrees and we had been driving directly into the sun for the previous four hours, with the five of us crammed into an un-air-conditioned 1941 Ford Business Coupe, converted to a sort of Club Coupe by the addition of seats from the junk yard — which almost fit.

When we finally reached Kilgore, I stopped to find a telephone, telling myself that if I couldn't locate him here, I would give up. I couldn't bear to torture my family any longer.

I found a listing in the phone book for Charles W. Rogers!

With trembling hands I dialed the number. A voice answered, stating that I had reached an automobile body shop. "Could I speak to Charles W. Rogers?" I asked.

"Oh, he ain't heah. He's ovah at Tyler."

That was the end for me. In a way I was relieved. I told the voice who I was and asked it to give my birth father the message that I had tried to find him.

The voice answered, "Oh, yuh shouldn't give up now. Tyler's only ten miles west of heah."

The voice gave me directions to where I could find him and his telephone number in Tyler. I hung up the phone and called my father. The call was not without emotion for me. I was talking to my birth father for the first time in my life. I kept the call brief because of emotion and told him I would be at the Packard dealership where he worked in twenty minutes.

During the ride over to Tyler I practiced in my mind several ways that I could tell him who I was, and finally settled on the best line. When we arrived I left my family in the air-conditioned showroom while I went to the back. Walking past several Packards in for repairs and body work, I approached a man who held a clipboard and seemed to be making an estimate on a car. All the ways I had practiced to introduce myself fled my mind. All I could do was extend my hand and say, "Hi, you must be my dad."

He reached and shook my hand. "Yeah, I guess I must be."

We spent the night and the following day with him, his wife and his four-year-old daughter. The wife was number four and the little girl was only his second child. Conversation with him was difficult because we had absolutely no reference points, no interests in common whatever.

At sundown we piled back in the coupe and headed north to Missouri. We'd had enough of daytime driving in the sweltering heat. The children fell asleep almost at once. My wife talked to me for a couple of hours, then she, too drifted off. I was left to drive all night, immersed in my thoughts. At sunrise I drove into St. Louis, almost exhausted from the long, tiring trip.

My birth father had given me the name of his sister and her husband. We made arrangements to meet at a restaurant for coffee. My aunt turned out to be unpleasant, but "Uncle Joe" Connors made up for her lack of warmth. He was a real class guy.

The real jewel was my Grandmother Mary, whom I met the next Saturday at their home. Her face had assumed the square shape of the typical older American Indian, but it had fewer lines than a white person. Her pure silver hair hung to her waist and so thick that it required double braiding. She spoke English very haltingly, but I could understand her pretty well. What I didn't understand could be made clear with a few hand signals and facial signs. These were the times that I saw tiny smiles on her face.

I came over at least once a week for the next three weeks, bringing wild game each time. She always cooked the game and we shared it. She told me the only things about my Grandfather Rogers that I ever learned. He had been dead several years by the time I was born.

Then my aunt destroyed our new-found happiness. Without advance warning she showed up at my front door, bringing along my birth father, an uncle and another friend. I invited them to wait inside while I ran to a store three doors away for some refreshments.

I had left the store and was walking back to my house when they roared past me without warning. I opened the door and found my wife crying and at the same time more furious than I had ever seen her.

When she calmed down enough that I could understand her, I learned that my aunt had brought them to determine if I really was a son of Charles William Rogers. As it happened, she said, only my birth father and my aunt had thought that I was not.

I waited a week to allow him time to return to Texas and then called him. I offered to pay for all the necessary blood tests, both for him and myself. "No," he curtly said, "that won't be necessary. No matter how it turns out, I'm already convinced."

In that forever-severing moment, I realized who my real father was. It was the man who loved me and who with never a single complaint had cared for my every need until I left home to join the Navy.

There had been times when I was rude to Dad. Times when I was even snotty. Times when I performed the few jobs he assigned me, in a sloppy way, so sloppy that many times he had to do them over. Until that final severance with my birth father, I had never really shown appreciation for all the things my real dad had done for me.

That changed. He lived for twenty-seven more years and I tried every day of those years to make up for my past shortcomings.

Dad was not one to talk of his own achievements. After he and Mother retired and moved to Sebring, Florida, I noticed in a newspaper that fifty years before Dr. O.J. Fritsch had invented the optical film projector. I cut the notice out of the paper and during my next visit with them in Florida, I asked him if he was related to the inventor. He read the article, smiled, and said, "I didn't think anybody would remember." He was so dedicated to his profession that he had given away all rights in return for the first machine ever produced.

He was my "real" father and I was privileged to have him and Mother come to live with us in his last years. Finally, I was forced to place him in a small nursing home near our house.

A few weeks later a nurse called to say he was declining fast. My wife, Laura and I raced to be at Dad's bedside. Mother was not dressed and said she would come as quickly as possible.

His eyes were dull when Laura and I arrived. I immediately leaned close and said, "Dad, I love you."

I think he heard me because there was a tiny smile on his lips when he died — just before Mother got there.

Two years later Mother died suddenly from a brain hemorrhage.

I — her only child — buried her at my father's side.

Now I am seventy and not in the best of health. Laura and I live in St. Charles, a small town west of St. Louis. The Lord gave us six children, of which four are still living. Keith, died in 1985 at age 41 and son John died in 1992.

The last time I counted, we had seventeen grandchildren. When they came to see us, memories of happy times with Daddy and Grandmother Floyd come rolling back.

I have lived a long time. In that time I have seen changes not only in the South but all across America. I have seen much of the morality of yesteryear disappear from the heart of America.

My wife, Laura, and I realized years ago that we must seek the best possible schooling for our children. While respecting the decisions of other parents to send their children to public schools, we decided to send our children to private schools. Then we home-schooled our youngest son, Ben.

Not everyone thought home schooling was a good idea for Ben. But after seeing him skip his senior year of high school, earn a scholarship to the college of our choice and score a perfect 4.0 average in his first semester, they changed their minds. This told us something we should have known all along: parents can best teach children values, principles and morality of the old America. All of our grandchildren, still in school, are now being schooled at home. For our efforts in establishing home-schooling in Missouri, Laura and I will be honored this June.

I was blessed by having a mother, step-father and grandparents who cared. They are now on the "other side" where I expect to join them and my Lord soon.

We'll have a lot to talk about, but I first intend to thank the Great Conductor for giving me guidance and safe passage through life.

Acknowledgments
and Thanks

Originally, I planned a series of stories for my seventeen grandchildren, to tell what life was like on a Mississippi red dirt farm in the 1920's and 30's without electric lights, appliances, television, radio, running water, toilets and toilet paper (thank God for the old Sears Roebuck catalogs). My beloved wife, Laura, then persuaded me to expand my stories into a book about the people and events that shaped my life.

Memory is a tool of the mind and not its slave. Shifting layers of time can distort the memory, much as heat waves over the desert alter the view of distant mountains. If some of my friends and loved ones have grown in stature over the years in the way I have depicted them, then I make no excuses. Love needs no apologies.

Some names have slipped from my pool of remembrances and I've taken the liberty of reconstructing them. In a few cases I've placed events in a historical context so the reader can relate to them better. Some events are second or even third hand and I wrote them the way I heard them and cannot vouch for absolute accuracy in every detail.

Some of the attitudes I present are controversial, but to hide or gloss over them would be dishonest. That about which I write is confined to my family, chums, friends and neighbors and should not be construed to be held by all Southern people of that time. Sometimes I'm blunt and opinionated because that's the way I am. Grandpas have rights too.

The events really did happen, but in many instances I had to fill in with dialogue and detail. No one can remember everything that ever happened or was spoken to them.

And the dialect is as was spoken in east central Mississippi in the 1920's and '30's.

Now I would like to say thanks to some very special people who made this book see the published light of day.

Next to God for His goodness and saving grace, I thank my dear wife, Laura, God's special gift to me. She has patiently listened, ad infinitum, to the tales of my boyhood recounted in this book. She has served as both cheerleader and writing coach, inciting confidence that sometime, somewhere my book would be published.

I thank Dr. James C. Hefley my publisher, editor, and in some instances my re-write man. Laura and I got to know Dr. Hefley by attending his seminar, "Writing for Publication," and by participating in the Mark Twain Writers Conference which he directs each year in Mark Twain's Hannibal. Jim Hefley believed my book had "possibilities" from the time he first saw a manuscript — four years ago. Following his suggestions, I wrote and rewrote, wrote and rewrote. Finally, he said, "Let me have your latest draft and we'll see what can be done with it."

Like me, Jim is a grandfather who grew up in the country. His boyhood story, *Way Back in the Hills*, is now in a thirteenth printing. He also spent his boyhood in Newton County, Arkansas.

I thank Cyndi Allison — Jim's daughter, chief "bear" catcher, and champion nit-picker. Cyndi checked the proofs, designed the cover, and drew the map showing all the important places of my Newton County childhood. Thank you, Cyndi.

There are many others I could thank, but it may be for the better that I don't. None of them — especially my aunts and uncles — deserve blame for mistakes that come from a faulty memory.

Country Classics
from Hannibal Books
Please send me

_____
In Care of the Conductor, by Jim Rogers

_____ Copies at $5.95 = _____

_____
Way Back in the Ozarks, by Howard Jean
Hefley & James C. Hefley. Stories of a boy
named "Monk," his dog & his coon.

_____ Copies at $5.95 = _____

_____
12 + Me by Pat Likes. "Pike County Patsie"
relives her childhood as the youngest of 13
children.

_____ Copies at $7.95 = _____

_____
Movin' Mountains by Lori Hann Evens. The
first book of The Pilgrimage introduces
Charity Lynne Waller.

_____ Copies at $7.95 _____

_____
*Please add $2.00 postage and handling for first
book, plus $.50 for each additional book.*

Shipping & Handling _____

MO residents add sales tax _____

TOTAL ENCLOSED _____

Name _____

Address _____

City _____ State ____ Zip _____

Mail coupon with check or money
order to: HANNIBAL BOOKS
921 Center
Hannibal, MO 63401

Call 800-747-0738 for quantity prices.
Satisfaction guaranteed.

More Country Classics
from Hannibal Books
Please send me...

Way Back in the Ozarks, Book 2 by Howard
Jean Hefley & James C. Hefley. "Ozark Monk"
relives the tale of Danny Boy.

_____ Copies at $5.95= _____

Way Back in the Ozarks, VHS VIDEO TAPE.
Meet "Ozark Monk" as he entertains you with
stories from his first book. Filmed on location.

_____Tapes at $15.95 = _____

Way Back in the 'Korn' Fields, by James C.
Hefley. Jokes that make Grandpa laugh
without making Grandma blush. Indexed
alphabetically by topic

_____Copies at $5.95= _____

Ozark Mountain Hymns, Audio Cassette
Tape features banjo, fiddle, dobro, mandolin &
acoustic guitar. New songs & old time favorites.

_____Tapes at $6.95 = _____

---

*Please add $2.00 postage and handling for first
book, plus $.50 for each additional book.*

Shipping & Handling _____

MO residents add 6.7% sales tax _____

TOTAL ENCLOSED _____

Name _____

Address _____

City _____ State ____Zip _____

Mail coupon with check or money
order to: HANNIBAL BOOKS
921 Center
Hannibal, MO 63401
Call 800-747-0738 for quantity prices.